Developing Learning Communities Through Teacher Expertise

Developing Learning Communities Through Teacher Expertise

Giselle O. Martin-Kniep

CORWIN PRESS
A Sage Publications Company
Thousand Oaks, California

For information:

Corwin Press
A Sage Publications Company
2455 Teller Road
Thousand Oaks, California 91320
www.corwinpress.com

Sage Publications Ltd.
6 Bonhill Street
London EC2A 4PU
United Kingdom

Sage Publications India Pvt. Ltd.
B-42, Panchsheel Enclave
Post Box 4109
New Delhi 110 017 India

Printed in the United States of America

Library of Congress Cataloging-in-Publication Data

Martin-Kniep, Giselle O., 1956-
Developing learning communities through teacher expertise / by Giselle Martin-Kniep.
    p. cm.
Includes bibliographical references (p.   ) and index.
ISBN 0-7619-4616-0—ISBN 0-7619-4617-9 (pbk.)
  1. Teachers—In-service training—United States. 2. Group work in education—United States.
3. Teachers—Professional relationships—United States. I. Title.
LB1731.M364 2004
370´.71´5—dc22

                                    2003016580

This book is printed on acid-free paper.

03   04   05   06   07   7   6   5   4   3   2   1

Acquisitions Editor:	Rachel Livsey
Editor at Large:	Mark Goldberg
Editorial Assistant:	Phyllis Cappello
Production Editor:	Julia Parnell
Copy Editor:	Elisabeth Magnus
Proofreader:	Theresa Kay
Typesetter:	C&M Digitals (P) Ltd.
Indexer:	Sylvia Coates
Cover Designer:	Michael Dubowe
Production Artist:	Lisa Miller

Contents

Preface   vii

Acknowledgments   xiii

About the Author   xv

1. Learning Communities   1

    What Are Learning Communities?   1

    Why Are They Important?   2

    What Do Learning Communities Do? What Do They Require to Function?   2

    What Gets in the Way of the Development of Learning Communities?   7

    What Can We Do to Support Learning Communities?   11

    Possible Questions for the Reader   13

    Recommended Books on Learning Communities   13

2. Standards-Based Curriculum and Assessment Design   15

    What Does It Take to Develop a Standards-Based,   29
        Learner-Centered Unit?

    How Do We Help Teachers Develop High-Quality
        Standards-Based Units?   30

    Possible Questions for the Reader   32

    Recommended Books on Standards-Based Curriculum and
        Assessment Design   32

3. Data-Driven Inquiry and Action Research   37

    Three Examples of Inquiry   38

    How Can Schools Support Individual, Collaborative, and
        School-Based Research?   56

    Possible Questions for the Reader   56

    Recommended Books on Action Research and Use of Data   57

4. Professional Portfolios   59

    What Do Professional Portfolios Include?   60

    Understanding and Use of Standards-Based and Learner-Centered
        Curriculum and Assessment   60

    Use of Reflection and Data to Improve One's Practice   66

    How Are Professional Portfolios Organized?

    How Can Schools   69

Begin to Support the Development and Use of Professional Portfolios? 75
Possible Questions for the Reader 76
Recommended Books on Portfolios 76

5. Developing an Action Plan **79**
Identification of Internal Expertise 79
Assessment of Needs 79
Brokering of Relationships Among Teachers 80
Curriculum and Assessment Design Work 81
Inquiry and Analysis Work 81
Professional Portfolio Work 82

Appendix A: Description of CSETL and Its Mission 83

Appendix B: Unit Design Template 85

Appendix C: Application to Become a CSETL Fellow 95

Appendix D: Professional Portfolio Rubric 97

References 101

Index 103

Preface

Internal capacity building, the effort to promote teachers as experts, is more than a buzzword. Most districts want it but do not know how to support it. Some districts are not certain that it is possible to develop it. Others have modestly developed it but do not know how to harness or expand it.

Capacity building is about enabling good teachers and administrators to share and disseminate their expertise in an environment that is both rigorous and supportive. It is about securing sufficient time and space for these educators to produce quality work and reflect on their practice. It is about developing learning communities where groups of teachers and administrators ponder and analyze students' work to identify and monitor their needs. It is about fostering shared leadership and creating expert teams that are able to tackle the complex aspects of schools, including the standards and tests required by a particular district or state.

This is not easy to do. Often schools do not function in ways that develop staff's capacity to learn and grow. Norms of individualism tend to prevail over collaborative problem solving and inquiry; innovations are adopted quickly but are seldom carried through implementation in any complete way; staff is divided into cliques; and administrative policies focus on short-term and immediate problems. Schools rely too much on outside experts, an expensive and not usually enduring way to develop teacher expertise.

The main premise of this book is that schools can engage in activities that support the development of learning communities by identifying and maximizing teachers' expertise. Learning communities are critical if schools want to increase their organizational capacity to improve student learning (Newmann, Secada, & Wehlage, 1995). These communities need to treat teachers and administrators as learners because such treatment has been linked to the creation of learning organizations (Argyris & Schon, 1978). When these activities are centered on standards-based curriculum and assessment design, data-driven inquiry, and portfolio development, they can enhance teachers' practices, increase student learning, and produce concrete and valuable school products and processes.

The book's chapters address four basic questions about capacity building:

1. How do we develop learning communities that embrace the notion of "teachers teaching teachers"?

2. How do we operationalize a standards-based and learner-centered curriculum so that all teachers will understand what it entails?

viii • Developing Learning Communities Through Teacher Expertise

3. How do we enable teachers to pursue questions of great significance about their practice?

4. How can we use professional portfolios as frameworks for documenting professional expertise?

In Chapter 1, I examine learning communities as a construct that has great potential but is very fragile. Teachers and the administrators who work with them must form active communities to build expertise, to examine important questions related to school life, and to nurture the permanent effort to help school communities keep questioning, learning, and growing. These communities are critical if any educational reform effort is to be sustained (Louis, Kruse, & Marks, 1996). Examples of learning communities and how they work are included.

In Chapter 2, I address standards-based curriculum and assessment design with particular emphasis on how to focus on standards with rigor and time-tested best practices (Newmann & Associates, 1996). I have included three specific teaching units and supporting material that illustrate the use of such practices and underscore the real expertise that some teachers have and that is worth cultivating in many more.

Chapter 3 examines action research and data-driven inquiry as processes that teachers and administrators can use to examine their practice through individual questions or through collaborative work. These processes are intrinsic to the cultivation of systematic inquiry and reflection, which, in turn, has a positive effect on teachers and students. Many questions can be addressed throughout the year, and this chapter will show how, exactly, to do this.

Chapter 4 looks at professional portfolios that reflect the complexity of teaching and the work of teachers. Understanding and honoring such complexity is important if we want to cultivate effective practice. Some attention is also paid to the work of administrators and in-house staff developers. The chapter addresses the materials that can be collected to aid educators in reflecting the richness of their practice. It also discusses the organizational structures and frameworks that can assist teachers and administrators in the development of their professional portfolios. Finally, it discusses strategies for using a portfolio as a tool for monitoring and improving professional decisions rather than as a document that stands separately from one's practice. Sample portfolio materials are shown and examined.

The final chapter provides some guidelines for the development of an action plan centered on the design of standards-based curriculum and assessment, individual and collaborative inquiry, and professional portfolios.

The material in this book is aimed at teachers, professional developers, and school administrators. Teachers can benefit from the frameworks, templates, and examples that support each of the chapters and use them to determine the value and implications surrounding the use of teacher-designed standards-based curriculum and assessment, data-driven inquiry, and professional portfolios.

Professional developers can use the material in the book to guide or refine their staff development activities and to consider the role of explicit reflection and ongoing documentation in the design and sustainability of teachers' work toward the goal of school improvement.

The book may be useful to school administrators who want to explore the conditions that are needed for teachers to develop quality materials and processes and the benefits that are derived from this endeavor.

These chapters are intended to serve as models for what groups of educators, not an individual teacher, can do to fill in the curriculum gap between standards we want for our students and the curriculum and instruction we use to support them. Figuring out how to create communities of adult learners, how to bring the standards alive, how to design rigorous and meaningful learning experiences, how to reflect on one's work, how to solve learning problems and overcome classroom obstacles, and how to work on all these things and more is the task teachers face. Unless we face this challenge, we will not get past business as usual in schools.

Each school or district must consider how best to use professional development time and money. Of course, some schools are more interested in portfolios, and others are more interested in standards-based design, action research, or something else. I well understand that the amount of time and money a district can devote to professional development will vary, but the days of no or little professional development are over. We now need to consider how to invest in professional development that produces the kinds of changes we want to see in classrooms. No school or district can rely on textbooks or commercial materials exclusively or even in large part if it is to be taken seriously about wanting rich curriculum to support the standards that have been established in the past 10 years. Nor can it rely on the typical 1 or 2 days for professional development aimed at all teachers but suited to none.

The material in this book is based on work completed in the past several years at the Center for the Study of Expertise in Teaching and Learning (CSETL), a nonprofit center whose mission is to identify, package, and disseminate teaching expertise. This center grew out of my work with many teachers who had participated in comprehensive professional development programs that I led from 1992 to 1997. In such programs, I discovered an unbelievable amount of talent that was mostly known and appreciated by the students who had the privilege of being taught by those who possessed it. Without legitimate career ladders where the expertise of teachers, administrative staff, and professional developers could be captured, shared, and disseminated, I had to create a forum that would honor what could be deemed the wisdom of practice. CSETL provides educators with a professional forum for collaborative research, development, and reflection. It also serves as a catalyst that enables its fellows to assume leadership positions within their districts and beyond. See Appendix A for more information about CSETL.

Environments such as the ones created by CSETL can exist in schools and can become part of the fabric of school life. However, unless more schools and districts appreciate the necessity to cultivate and honor the expertise of those who teach, we will need to support more expensive and less accurately targeted organizations that are committed to identifying, packaging, and disseminating general best practice.

The overarching essential question of the book is "Can we develop a school's capacity to become a learning community?" In light of the historically poor use of externally driven professional development for teachers, I believe we cannot afford not to.

This book proposes that capacity building is possible and that it may be cultivated within a segment of a school or as a schoolwide endeavor. My approach is guided by four assumptions:

1. *Schools can become better at identifying and using their own professional expertise.*

Professional development is, in most districts, a commodity in short supply. It is an insignificant percentage of a school's budget and is too often poorly linked to the specific needs of teachers who receive it. Professional development that is imported from the outside can, at its best, introduce new ideas and mobilize the beginnings of change. The more typical professional development scenario is the introduction of new ideas and skills without the appropriate support mechanisms to implement them. Studies have shown that staff development activities undertaken in isolation from teachers' ongoing classroom responsibilities rarely have much impact on teaching practices or on student learning (Doyle & Ponder, 1977; Guskey & Sparks, 1996). To have an impact on practice, professional development programs must offer teachers ways of building on and refining their practices to directly enhance desired learning outcomes in students.

What is required is an initial solid introduction to a new concept or skill followed by ongoing and job-embedded professional development sessions over time. There is increasing evidence (Bain & Jacobs, 1990; Stronge, 2002) that high-quality professional development activities are necessary tools for improving teaching effectiveness and that teacher effectiveness is positively correlated to increased student learning (Brophy & Good, 1986; Collinson, Killeavy, & Stephenson, 1999; Covino & Iwanicki, 1996; Cruickshank & Haefele, 2001; Mitchell, 1998; Rowan, Chiang, & Miller, 1997). Effective teachers appear to be effective with students of all achievement levels, regardless of the level of heterogeneity in their classrooms (Wright, Horn, & Sanders, 1997).

Professional development activities are most effective when they are collegial and challenging because learning itself involves these characteristics. Staff development programs concerning new programs and innovations are most successful when teachers can regularly discuss their experiences in an atmosphere of collegiality and experimentation. For most teachers, having the opportunity to share perspectives and seek solutions to common problems is extremely beneficial (Little, 1981).

There are teachers in every school with well-developed talents. In some cases, these talents are modest and focused, as in knowing how to help students take notes in different ways. In others, they are broad and more significant, as in the case of teachers who know and can develop different kinds of learning experiences for students with a wide range of needs. Rarely is a teacher an expert in every area. However, if schools knew and sought to identify different kinds of expertise among their teaching staff, they would probably find that they had much of the expertise they needed, or at least a lot more than what they thought they had. For the rest, small teams of teachers can be prepared by experts and can then, in turn, share their expertise with the rest of the staff via study groups, collegial circles, or action research endeavors.

2. *Standards-based design is an effective means of revisiting, improving, and refining curriculum, instruction, and assessment.*

The advent of standards at the state and national levels has provided schools with the opportunity to revisit teachers' curriculum and assessment practices that may otherwise remain unchanged. Standards can easily become the catalyst that enables teachers in different grades and subjects to identify what is essential and discard old baggage.

Standards-based design is efficient and parsimonious (Martin-Kniep, 2000; Wiggins & McTighe, 1998). By designing backwards, teachers can identify specific standards and indicators from different content areas and then select lessons and assessments that directly relate to and support students' learning and attainment of these standards. Over time, they can reorganize what originally may be perceived as a wide range of disparate and unconnected content into a relatively small number of well-organized units.

The opportunity to carefully consider standards as the foundation for design enables teachers to make meaningful connections between curriculum, instruction, and assessment and, in so doing, to articulate their teaching to maximize student learning.

3. *A significant wealth of knowledge about teaching and learning is best understood by those who teach every day, namely classroom teachers.*

Teachers understand and experience the learning process from within. They face the uncertainties of learning when an apparently well-thought-out set of activities is misunderstood by the students who experience it; when, in answering a question, students make unrelated connections and acquire surprising insights; or when students demonstrate profound insights about fairly new content.

Given the appropriate conditions, teachers can greatly inform what we know about how and when students learn. In fact, there is growing evidence (Stiegler & Herbert, 1999) that if we truly want to improve schools, teachers must be at the heart of change efforts. "Not only are they the gatekeepers for all improvement efforts, they are also in the best position to acquire the knowledge that is needed. They are, after all, the only ones who can improve teaching" (p. 174).

Other scholars (Fullan, 1994; Guskey, 1986; Marantz Cohen, 2002) assert that without a deeper and broader conceptualization of teacher leadership, efforts to develop it in schools will fail.

The conditions that support the development and use of teachers' expertise include the opportunity for teachers to investigate their own practice using action research and other forms of systematic inquiry. They also include the opportunity for teachers to engage in collaborative discourse around issues of substance, as well as ponder such essential questions about teaching and learning as the following:

1. What content and skills are essential? What content and skills are expendable?

2. How do we identify, use, and adapt the most appropriate curriculum, assessment, and instructional strategies to address the needs of increasingly diverse learners?

3. How do we balance the need to help students do well on state and other standardized tests without compromising curriculum integrity?

Learning communities can be created by educators who exercise leadership in the design, investigation, and dissemination of their expertise and who actively participate in their own learning process. These educators may include teachers, professional developers, administrators, and university professors. According to Swanson (2000), these leaders employ five practices. They (a) challenge the process; (b) inspire a shared vision; (c) enable others to act; (d) model the way; and (e) encourage the heart. These are key characteristics of dynamic learning communities.

4. *Professional portfolios legitimize and validate teachers' expertise.*

Teaching involves a range of skills, content expertise, and dispositions that requires a multifaceted documentation system. Such a system should allow for the documentation of teaching processes, performances, and products. Professional portfolios can support this system. They can also offer teachers a vehicle for shaping and personalizing the documentation and analysis of their thinking processes and professional values. By enabling teachers and other educators to explicitly reflect on their practice, portfolios can play a critical role in enhancing professional change. Theorists of adult learning have emphasized reflection as a means of achieving transformative learning and more radical approaches to the curriculum and its outcomes (Boud, Keogh, & Walker, 1985; Boud & Walker, 1998; Thomas & Montgomery, 1998).

Portfolios need to strike a balance between being comprehensive and being realistic. They cannot be so burdensome that teachers simply won't do them or find them helpful. When portfolios are used to document as well as share knowledge, thinking processes, and accomplishments, they can provide a means for capturing professional decisions, goals, and questions that often remain hidden or unrecognized. In a sense, portfolios can become the filing and organizing system for design and inquiry activities. In addition, they can uncover the processes surrounding such activities and the thinking behind them.

Acknowledgments

This book was inspired by a need to disseminate the ideas and work of many teachers and administrators who believe, as I do, that teachers have much to say about effective teaching and learning. Primary among these are the following educators whose work is included in this book (all are based in New York State):

Jeanette Atkinson, Genesee Valley Board of Cooperative Educational Services (BOCES)

Elizabeth Bedell, William Floyd School District

Lisa Boerum, Sag Harbor School District

Barbara Colton, Learner-Centered Initiatives

Vicki DeRue, Gates-Chili School District

Angela DiMichele Lalor, Learner-Centered Initiatives

Shirley Glickman, Community School District 10

Kristin Kendall-Jakus, Genesee Valley BOCES

Linda Hughs, private consultant

Patricia Lynch, Manhasset School District

Lisa McEvoy, Mattituck-Cutchogue School District

Karen Palmerini, Jennifer Pasqua, and Jennifer's fourth graders, Middle Country School District

Alex Papadopoulos, Mattituck-Cutchogue School District

Joanne Picone-Zocchia, Learner-Centered Initiatives

Anne Smith, Mattituck-Cutchogue School District

Carol M. Varsalona, Reading Specialist, Freeport Public Schools

I would like to thank the many educators who have supported my work in schools over the past 10 years. Among these are Mark Bower, Kathy Gilmore, Stephanie Krusa, Joan Daly-Lewis, and Jo Slovak.

I am also indebted to my friend and colleague Diane Cunningham for helping me support CSETL and for helping its fellows find their voice.

Thanks to Mark Goldberg for being a thoughtful editor and caring friend.

Thanks to Diana Muxworthy Feige for joining forces with me in pursuit of a place that will support and nurture teachers' expertise.

Last but not least, I need to acknowledge Rick Hinrichs, who during the time I wrote this book was not only a contributor to it but also a patient reader, reviewer, editor, partner, and friend.

The contributions of the following reviewers are gratefully acknowledged:

Doug Fisher
Associate Professor of Teacher Education
San Diego State University
San Diego, CA

Cheryl Sullivan
Staff Developer
Decatur, GA

Catherine Payne
Principal
W. R. Farrington High School
Honolulu, HI

Suzanne "Chris" Fonoti
Principal
Cromer Elementary School
Flagstaff Unified School District
Flagstaff, AZ

Mark Bower
Director of Staff Development
Hilton Central School District
Hilton, NY

Richard Strong
Vice President
Silver Strong & Associates
Ho-Ho-Kus, NJ

About the Author

Giselle Martin-Kniep is a teacher educator, researcher, program evaluator, and writer. She is the president of Learner-Centered Initiatives, Ltd., an educational consulting organization specializing in comprehensive regional and school-based curriculum and assessment work. She is also the CEO of the Center for the Study of Expertise in Teaching and Learning, an organization committed to the discovery and dissemination of teacher expertise.

Dr. Martin-Kniep has a strong background in organizational change and has graduate degrees in communication and development, social sciences in education, and educational evaluation from Stanford University. She has taught at Adelphi University, the University of British Columbia, and the University of Victoria. In the last fourteen years, she has worked with hundreds of schools and districts nationally and internationally in the areas of alternative assessment, standards-based design, school change, and action research.

To all the CSETL fellows who work so hard to create tangible evidence of their expertise, passion, and commitment to the profession

Learning Communities

We have learned that teaching is not a simple skill but rather a complex cultural activity that is highly determined by beliefs and habits that work partly outside the realm of consciousness.

—J. W. Stiegler and J. Herbert, *The Teaching Gap*

WHAT ARE LEARNING COMMUNITIES?

Teaching is, for the most part, a lonely act. Teachers and administrators spend much of their workdays directing or enabling other people's learning and work. Their interactions with adults are limited to brief exchanges or to problem-solving and classroom management situations. "In many cases, teachers share the same feelings of alienation in school that students do. Teacher isolation has permeated schools for decades. Teachers work in their individual classrooms with little time to interact and connect with other adults" (Combs, Miser, & Whitaker, 1999, p. 140).

Learning communities are the means by which we can break such isolation and foster a collaborative and reflective culture. In fact, creating a collaborative environment has been described as "the single most important factor" for successful school improvement initiatives and "the first order of business" for those seeking to enhance the effectiveness of their school (Eastwood & Lewis, 1992, p. 215).

Learning communities can be large or small. They can work within formal structures of collaboration, inquiry, and reflection or can operate loosely. They are composed of teacher leaders who have a shared commitment to teacher, school, or student learning, common goals, or a unified vision. This vision of leadership is consistent with that of Kouzes and Posner (1999), who defined leadership as the art of mobilizing and inspiring others to struggle for shared aspirations.

In this chapter, I pursue the question of how we develop learning communities that embrace the notion of "teachers teaching teachers" by using the experiences we have amassed at the Center for the Study of Expertise in Teaching and Learning (CSETL) to show the power of learning communities in stimulating individual learning and organizational change. In 1995, CSETL began with a group of 15 teachers, all of whom had been identified through work my colleagues and I were doing in the New York City metropolitan area. Each year, CSETL fellows met for 7 full days during the year and for 1 week each summer. Most of the teachers we recruited were eager and curious learners who had acquired significant expertise in standards-based design, portfolio assessment, or action research. Though they experienced much success with their students, they were hungry for learning opportunities that would challenge them as adult learners and help them grow as teachers.

The mechanisms we have used to cultivate learners and to create a learning community can be used in school buildings or school districts as long as there is an overall climate where risk taking is encouraged and celebrated. We have proof of their applicability in that we now have teams of administrators and teachers who replicate in their own schools what they have done in CSETL. Anne Smith, the principal of Cutchogue East Elementary School, in Cutchogue, Long Island, New York, addresses this process:

> Ultimately, it is the process of CSETL that is becoming a part of the culture of the school, using CSETL as a model for how teachers and administrators can work together. The process has a profound impact on the quality of instruction so that we think of curriculum embedded assessment programs, not just isolated content we want to teach.

WHY ARE THEY IMPORTANT?

Learning communities are important because they help teachers move away from the immediacy of quick decisions and actions, thus enabling them to ponder questions about how to improve teaching or maximize learning. They also foster collaborative environments that create positive working relationships and help retain teachers.

Learning communities facilitate the exchange of ideas and the use of feedback to improve professional practices. The research on effective teaching indicates that effective teachers elicit information and criticism from others. "Additionally, in the interest of improving their ability to have a positive impact on student learning, these teachers readily accept constructive criticism and reflect upon it" (Stronge, 2002, p. 21).

Learning communities are essential if we are seeking to cultivate the internal capacity of schools to support their continued improvement. In the absence of learning communities, schools must rely exclusively on outside experts for their improvement. Not only is this costly, but it denies the validity of using current staff to determine what needs to be improved in a school and to select the best solutions or strategies to address those needs. There is too much one-shot staff development that seldom becomes fully implemented, let alone institutionalized (Doyle & Ponder, 1977; Guskey, 1986). A learning community culture is necessary for long-lasting change in teachers' beliefs and practices. There are no alternatives to sustained and focused attention on the development of teachers' knowledge and skills if we want to improve schools.

WHAT DO LEARNING COMMUNITIES DO?
WHAT DO THEY REQUIRE TO FUNCTION?

Learning communities engage in a wide range of activities centered on teaching and learning. These activities include individual and collaborative curriculum development projects, the review and analysis of student work, teachers' presentations to their peers and others, action research and collaborative inquiry activities, and collaborative reflective work. All of these activities are most effective in an environment where participants share the following beliefs and behaviors:

- Caring deeply about learning
- Feeling free to take risks
- Challenging each other and raising the expectations for everyone
- Respecting and valuing perspectives other than their own by seeking and valuing each other's input
- Asking questions of themselves and each other, even if the answers are sometimes elusive

These activities are supported by current research on teacher leadership. In a 2-year study of teacher leaders, Swanson (2000) found that teacher leaders challenge the process, inspire a shared vision, enable others to act, model the way, and encourage the heart. When leaders do their best to encourage the heart, they set clear standards, expect the best, pay attention, personalize recognition, tell the story, celebrate together, and set the example.

At CSETL, we promote the preceding behaviors through formal and informal processes. For example, to challenge the process, stimulate teachers' curiosity for learning, and develop a shared vision, we take time to ponder essential questions such as: What are the non-negotiables of teaching and learning? What aspects of teachers' expertise are learned while teaching? What are the best ways of gaining and transferring expertise? We discuss these questions, not in search of a definitive answer, but to make our assumptions explicit and to explore the different perspectives we possess as a group. Though these questions may not result in tangible products or processes, they nourish our intellect and force us to delve into our core values and beliefs. Faculty meetings and superintendent conference days would be well served by conversations around essential matters.

CSETL also encourages teachers to develop and publish original standards-based curriculum and assessment prototypes. All fellows are expected to publish a prototype over a 2- to 3-year period. Prototypes can be integrated standards-based units with accompanying assessments, year-long student portfolio designs, action research projects, staff development programs, or program evaluation studies.

CSETL prototype units, such as the ones described in Chapter 2, incorporate critical components of learner-centered, standards-rich curriculum and assessment, including (a) essential and guiding questions that launch and sustain student inquiry throughout the learning experience; (b) standards and indicators from at least two content areas that legitimize the unit's purpose and space within the overall curriculum; (c) integrated learning and assessment opportunities that consider a range of developmental needs and interests and provide teachers with ongoing feedback about students' learning; (d) rigor and inquiry to support the need for students to see themselves as researchers as well as active learners immersed in the process of making meaning of new information; (e) authentic culminating assessments that provide a real audience and purpose for students' work; and (f) reflective and evaluative opportunities that enhance strategic thinking and self-monitoring.

Schools can benefit from supporting individual and collaborative design work aimed at addressing specific classroom, grade, or program needs. I suggest, however, that unlike the fairly typical summer curriculum projects that many schools promote, any design work be accompanied by a quality review and feedback process whereby teachers assess their products against explicit design standards and continuously revise their work to address diverse student needs.

A crucial component of the CSETL process is the forming of groups that work together over time. The members can get to know each other, constantly frame specific agendas for rigorous and useful work, and produce materials for classrooms that are aligned with local standards and excellent pedagogy.

Fellows begin this process by exploring their professional strengths and interests and linking these to their practices. They brainstorm organizing centers or research questions and begin to outline the parameters for their standards-based unit, staff development module, or action research. Much of the prewriting occurs in the first year of CSETL, so writing activities begin in a fellow's first summer. More often than not, the drafting process takes 6 to 10 additional months, and the prototype is piloted and revised many times in between. Most prototypes are published 2 years after they are begun.

We have created a number of templates to assist fellows in the design process. Appendix B shows one of our most recent templates for the development of standards-based units. School administrators may find this template valuable in helping individuals or groups of teachers who are interested in developing or refining their curriculum.

Though most program fellows receive inservice credit for their work, the deeper rewards for fellows are the opportunity to work on projects that are of personal significance, the ongoing access to a cadre of individuals who are equally committed to their work, and the collective pursuit of wisdom and quality thinking. In many schools or districts, after a couple of years' experience, fellows play a leading role in staff development.

Fellows seek and value each other's input through formal processes such as mentoring and buddy arrangements. Through the mentoring process, experienced fellows help probationary and new fellows become part of the organization and community. As is consistent with research by Snell and Swanson (2000), we believe that mentors enhance knowledge acquisition and teach profound lessons about paying attention to human needs. This relationship exists formally for a period of 1 year.

To be considered a mentor, an experienced fellow must have designed, implemented, revised, and published a standards-based curriculum and assessment prototype. Mentors are matched with one to three probationary fellows on the basis of common interests and areas of expertise. Their primary objective is to assist their mentees in completing their baseline portfolio (see Appendix C) and help them begin to think through possibilities for prototype development. They will be the first readers of the portfolio and will, when it is submitted, participate in an assessment of their mentees' readiness for appointment as fellows.

The mentoring process involves exchanging ideas and questions by phone or e-mail or during formally scheduled sessions. Mentors ask mentees questions such as:

1. Where are you in the process of developing your baseline portfolio? What kind of assistance or support, if any, can I provide?

2. What are you struggling with?

3. How are you changing as a curriculum and assessment developer as a result of your CSETL work?

Mentees, in turn, use the mentors as critical friends and resources to negotiate their roles within the organization. They are responsible for responding within 48 hours to mentor communications.

CSETL relies on the mentoring process to help all fellows set reasonable goals for their research and development work during meetings as well as assess the extent to which those goals are addressed and attained.

In a school, a similar mentoring process can be established between new and veteran teachers, or between teachers who are just learning a specific program or curriculum and those who designed it or have used it for years. Such a process is also useful in transferring the experiences acquired by the best teachers who are close to retirement to those who are just beginning their teaching careers. Some schools already have some kind of mentoring and peer coaching process that could be refined to support teachers in the ways I have described.

Another mechanism that schools can use to promote meaningful sharing and dissemination of all teachers' experience and areas of expertise is a database. The work schedules and routines of teachers are such that frequently teachers lack information about what their colleagues know and do. Often this is evident in my work as a consultant when I begin to meet individual teachers and "discover" teachers who already have the specific knowledge and skills that a principal or some teachers have requested of me. A sample database on expertise is included in Table 1.1. Of course, databases can be more detailed and should be followed by small-group meetings.

To promote inquiry and reflective practice, CSETL encourages teachers to engage in individual, school-based, and collaborative research activities such as the ones described in Chapter 3. It also expects fellows to develop a professional portfolio and to use it as a mechanism to systematically reflect upon their practice. Two of the outcomes documented by this portfolio are described in Chapter 4. The entire portfolio rubric is found in Appendix D.

The preceding behaviors and processes work best in a context where challenging work is the norm. One of the primary activities used by CSETL includes the review and analysis of student work and of its relationship to teachers' practices. One effective protocol involves identifying the specific knowledge, skills, and standards that are evident in a student work sample, followed by identifying the specific learning needs exhibited by the work. The protocol ends with teachers brainstorming and prioritizing ideas and strategies for addressing such needs.

In schools, the analysis of student work can be conducted using existing protocols (Allen, 1998; Blythe, Allen, & Powell, 1999; Carini, 2001; Seidel, 1998) or can be done through a process designed by the people carrying out such review. What matters is that the review process connects the work of students with the instructional and assessment demands teachers make, so that the resulting analysis and conclusions have an impact on teachers' practices.

A second activity that supports the work of learning communities is the sharing and presentation of individual teachers' ideas and work. Though this often occurs in an informal fashion, it is important to create legitimate opportunities for teachers to examine and share their own work. Such opportunities communicate that the work is valued and that people in schools have something worthy to contribute to other adults in the building, in the district, or at educational conferences. In schools, administrators could encourage teachers to use the school or district conference days as a forum in which teachers could learn from each other either from work in individual classrooms or from work that has been the focus of a collegial circle or study group.

We encourage fellows to make a presentation at our annual conference as soon as they are ready to share the focus of their curriculum or research work. Even though the work that

Table 1.1   Simple Database

CSETL	Expertise	Experience With Workshops/Topics	Prototype

Vicki De Rue	K-12 writing
	Rubrics
	Curriculum writing
		Staff development on writing
		Integration of technology,
		  content areas, and writing
		  assessment tools
		Curriculum writing
		Document-based questions
		Use of assessment data to
		  improve instruction
			Why Do Writers Write?

Donata (Dee)
  Fulgione
	Developing expertise in
	  literature circles with
	  struggling readers
	Checklists
	Constructivist approach to
	  mathematics instruction
		Study groups: literature
		  circles
			Action Research on the
			  Effectiveness of Literature
			  Circles With Struggling
			  Readers

Iris Gandler	Teacher portfolios
	Student-led parent
	  conferences
	Action research
	Block planning/unit
	  development
	Co-teaching
	Reflection (student)
	Independent reading
	Rubric development
		Collegial planning
		MI and the arts
		Document-based question
		  development
		Student-led parent-teacher
		  conference
		Inclusion: a collaborative
		  approach
			Human Rights

is showcased may not be completed, the staff work with each fellow to ensure that these presentations embody all of the attributes of a learner-centered environment. Fellows use these presentations as an opportunity to test the merits of their thinking and to solicit feedback from colleagues outside our learning community. Though most fellows take advantage of the opportunity to present at conferences, no one is put in the position of having to make a presentation unless he or she is ready to assume that role. All presenters are provided with coaching and multiple opportunities for peer feedback as they prepare their session.

Some workshops that have been presented by fellows are

"Standards-Based Assessment Design"

"Using Reflection With Students"

"Goal Setting, Learner Portfolios, and Student-Led Conferences"

"Teacher as Designer: What Does It Look Like?"

"Integrating the Arts in Social Studies"

"Traveling the Rubric Road"

"Strategies for Communicating Mathematically"

"Supporting Teacher Growth"

"Student-Led Conferences"

"ABC: 123 Tools for Linking the Standards to the Primary Curriculum"

"Teaming to Meet the Standards"

"Yes, They Can!"

Whether or not a fellow presents at the conference, it is expected that all fellows will attend their colleagues' workshops. Participating in these workshops gives everyone the opportunity to learn and provides presenters with critical friends who can give feedback. Because of this, the presentations become learning opportunities for both presenters and participants. To assist fellows, we use rubrics such as the one in Table 1.2. Schools can use these rubrics and other self-assessment tools to help teachers self- and peer-assess.

The opportunity to present one's work to colleagues can lead to significant learning for both presenter and attendees. Following is a reflective entry from a teacher after carefully reviewing the feedback from program participants.

> Wouldn't it be wonderful if all feedback was positive! We could spend our days feeling good about ourselves. I made some mistakes. I will be better prepared next time. My presentations will be far less scripted. . . . Next time I use material that is not my own, I'll know it just as well as my own. I am an inexperienced presenter, but I'm getting experience. Presenting is not a piece of cake; it's hard work that demands meticulous attention to detail and extensive background knowledge.

The self-assessment rubric (Table 1.3) was developed to provide participants in professional development groups with an opportunity to assess their own level of engagement and learning.

As with the analysis of student work, this review can be enhanced through the use of formal protocols that define the boundaries of the feedback. We have used a protocol for peer review that fellows have found to be very valuable. In fact, many of them have used the same protocol with students. Table 1.4 is a description of this protocol.

The value of constructive feedback is tremendous for producing new learning. The following example from a teacher speaks for its value:

> If all the feedback I received were positive, future presentations would deteriorate. I suppose it is like anything else once you find a comfort zone. Initially, I chose to protect myself when I read the negative comments. It was so much nicer reading the positive, great food for the ego. Now I understand that negative comments are more useful for analysis and self-improvement. If you are honest with yourself and see any truth in the comments, it can help you grow and ultimately reach higher levels.

WHAT GETS IN THE WAY OF THE DEVELOPMENT OF LEARNING COMMUNITIES?

Much that goes on in schools gets in the way of learning communities. Beginning with tight schedules that leave little time for adult learning and collaboration and ending with environments that foster compliance rather than curiosity, schools rarely operate as if they understood or cared about community.

Table 1.2   Rubric for Professional Development Presentations

PROGRAM _____

Dimension	1	2	3	4	Rating/Notes
Engagement with audience	Workshop is based exclusively on presenter's purposes. Workshop is self-contained with no built-in opportunity for follow-up.	Presenter inquires about audience's needs but minimally adjusts workshop. Presenter acknowledges audience's experiences and backgrounds. Presenter offers limited resources for future learning and access.	Presenter inquires about the audience's backgrounds, experiences, and needs. Presenter articulates how those needs can be met. Presenter asks for questions at the end of the session. Presenter provides a list of resources (materials, people, sessions) for continued learning.	Presenter develops and co-constructs the session from the audience's needs. Presenter builds on and expands prior background and experiences. Presenter provides a broad menu of experiences and materials to extend learning and articulates next steps for the audience.	
Content	Ideas are inaccurate, outdated, or lacking research base and practical application. Presentation is unrealistic and unfocused and lacking balance between research and practice. Workshop does not include models or samples. Language is jargon-filled and inappropriate.	Ideas have little practical application. Topic is somewhat dated. Presenter addresses topic but with limited scope and research. Workshop includes presentation of models/samples. Language includes jargon that is not clearly defined.	Ideas are adaptable across a narrow range of grade levels and subjects. Topic is focused, accurate, and current. Presenter achieves a balance of theory and practice. Ideas are demonstrated through samples and modeling. Language is clear and understandable; terms are defined when necessary.	Presenter inspires and stimulates desire to gain additional knowledge. Ideas are immediately adaptable to individual needs and situations. Workshop is tightly focused on topic. Presenter seamlessly incorporates a balance of current and relevant research and practice. Workshop contains multiple demonstrations or samples from different settings/grades/subjects and ability levels. Language is well suited to target audience.	

(Continued)

8

Table 1.2   (Continued)

PROGRAM _____

Dimension	1	2	3	4	Rating/Notes
Delivery system and use of time	Lecture is focused on the delivery of material. There is no interaction between presenter and audience or among participants. Delivery plan is rigid. There is no time for reflection.	Workshop is mostly lecture, with isolated moments for interaction in the form of questions and answers at the end of session. Limited time is provided for interaction among participants. The delivery plan allows for some internalization of material, but there is no explicit time for reflection.	There are a variety of different activities that meet different styles and needs. Audience is actively involved in learning for a significant amount of time through questions and answers. There are opportunities for meaningful interactions between the presenter and the audience, and participants work in small and large groups. Pace is flexible and appropriate to content and audience. Time is provided for reflection at the end of the program.	Activities are specifically designed for the audience's learning needs. Participants are actively involved in learning throughout the program through a variety of activities. There are multiple opportunities for meaningful interaction among participants and between audience and participants. There is a balance between individual and collaborative learning. Opportunities for reflection are provided throughout the program.	
Media and handouts	No media or handouts are used, or those used are irrelevant. Presenter is the only medium.	Handouts require constant translation and explanation from the presenter to be useful. Media are limited to prescribed posters or visuals with which the presenter does not interact directly.	Handouts summarize material presented and are used as a reference or resource. Media include overheads, boards, or charts that are used in conjunction with the presentation.	Handouts assist in the understanding or processing of the material during the presentation and can be used as a resource afterwards. Use of media enhances the overall presentation or delivery.	

(Continued)

Table 1.2 (Continued)

PROGRAM _____

STRENGTHS	AREAS FOR IMPROVEMENTS
SPECIAL CIRCUMSTANCES/COMMENTS	CHANGES FOR NEXT PROGRAM

Table 1.3   Self-Assessment Rubric for Program Participants

	1 *Frustrated*	*2* *Unsure*	*3* *Engaged*	*4* *Eager*
Connection to self	I do not see the connection or relevance to me.	I believe there is a connection, but I cannot describe it.	This fits into what I know and do.	This validates and extends what I know and do.
Outlook/vision	I see no relationship between where I am and what is in front of me.	I recognize that there may be new possibilities, resources, or perspectives, but I cannot identify them.	I have identified and am interested in seeing and using new possibilities, resources, or perspectives to extend what I already know.	I can see and do old things in a new way.
Empowerment	I feel incapable of doing this.	I am willing to do this with direct guidance and support.	I am able to do this more or less on my own without direct instruction.	I am able to do this independently and guide someone else through the process.
Affect	My confusion and anxiety are overpowering. I will either shut down or resist.	I am aware of my discomfort and need help in working through believing that this is worth it.	I am comfortable with my discomfort. I know I can work through the fear.	I anticipate and use my fear and discomfort as a welcomed opportunity to be stretched.

Source: Designed by the CSETL Staff Development Ad Hoc Interest Group.

Teachers themselves can sabotage the incipient efforts of administrators to create learning communities because, historically, such efforts have been shallow and short-lived.

WHAT CAN WE DO TO SUPPORT LEARNING COMMUNITIES?

Much can be done to support learning communities. Administrators can begin by gathering data on the existing expertise on their faculty and finding ways to acknowledge and disseminate that expertise to all staff. Reminding everyone that no one is good at everything and that a good school should cultivate the specific talent that every teacher brings helps maximize the effects of a database. Having identified staff's expertise, administrators can create informal (e.g., voluntary bagel breakfasts once per week) and formal (superintendent's conference day) structures for showcasing, sharing, discussing, and extending such expertise.

Administrators or groups of teachers should also consider creating forums that encourage collegial work, study groups, or action research projects. To the extent that it is possible, it is worthwhile to focus these forums on specific school needs that have been identified by the entire school faculty, or at least a majority. Teachers who participate in these forums should be compensated for their time and effort with credit, release time, stipends, or some other compensation.

Table 1.4   Protocol for Peer Review

In peer review, participants present an idea, a piece of their work, or a question they're interested in exploring. Acting as "critical friends," members of the peer review group give "warm" feedback (feedback that validates the author by providing extensions, examples, or applications or by stating the ways in which the work is effective, relevant, or accurate) and "cool" feedback (feedback that helps the author refine or expand the work in the form of questions and confusions), helping the presenter to make new connections and see additional possibilities.

GUIDELINES FOR PEER REVIEW

Format

4–5 people in a group (preferably people who have not worked together)

- Round robin
- If someone agrees with someone else's feedback, he/she can ditto
- If someone wants to build on someone else's feedback, he/she can "piggyback"
- If someone has nothing to say, he/she can pass

Procedure

- Begin with one or more rounds of warm feedback until you've exhausted it.
- Proceed with one or more rounds of cool feedback until you've exhausted it.
- The person receiving feedback <u>cannot</u> respond to it but can take notes.
- When everyone in the group has received feedback, people can seek clarification or discuss feedback received.

Warm Feedback

- No praise
- Focus on relevance, applicability, and possibilities
  Examples:
  You can also address *x* with that . . .
  This could also be combined with . . .
  This might allow your students to understand . . .
  If you included the *x* teacher, you could also . . .

Cool Feedback

- No negative judgments
- Focus on questions and confusions
  Examples:
  I don't understand . . .
  Why did you . . . ?
  Could *x* have a negative effect on . . . ?

Schools would be well served if they devoted some of their resources to supporting teachers' learning via conferences, graduate work, national teacher accreditation, or comprehensive professional development aimed at simultaneously improving knowledge and practice. Even though this sounds undemocratic, it is by far more cost-effective to devote substantial resources to the development of a small cadre of teachers than to continue to invest all staff development funds in 1-day programs that everyone attends but from which little is gained.

Finally, administrators may want to consider sending an individual or a team of teachers to CSETL or a CSETL-like environment because sometimes one has to fully experience a learning community before attempting to create one.

As is the case with classrooms, learning communities emerge naturally from a climate of trust and caring in which the invitation to take risks is ever-present. In such communities, the pursuit of personally owned knowledge and the application of known skills in novel ways are explicitly valued. Discoveries are celebrated, and mistakes are considered valuable learning opportunities. These communities can be small or large, but they must always be composed of educators who care about each other, who value the process as well as the product, and who feel respected and safe.

POSSIBLE QUESTIONS FOR THE READER

1. Are there adult learning communities in your school or district? If yes, whom do they include? If no, where would you begin to create one or more?

2. Who are the teacher experts in your school or district?

3. What are the formal or informal mechanisms that your school or district uses to capitalize on the expertise of its teachers? If none exist, what could you do to begin to create these mechanisms?

RECOMMENDED BOOKS ON LEARNING COMMUNITIES

Blythe, T., Allen, D., & Powell, B. S. (1999). *Looking together at student work: A companion guide to "Assessing student learning."* New York: Teachers College Press.

> This book provides a process-centered approach to student work as a tool for moving toward goals and addressing the changes facing schools in light of educational reform. Work actually done in several schools using this approach is shared along with step-by-step explanations of several models or protocols that can be adapted for use in individual schools.

Combs, A. W., Miser, A. B., & Whitaker, K. S. (1999). *On becoming a school leader: A person-centered challenge.* Alexandria, VA: Association for Supervision and Curriculum Development.

> This book discusses the many facets of being a school leader. It is divided into three sections: "Leadership and Belief Systems," "Leaders' Conceptions of Change and Self," and "Leaders and Organizations." The authors provide the reader with a clear understanding of what makes an effective administrator and of some challenges that a school administrator might encounter. The scenarios are especially helpful in letting the reader connect theory with practice.

DuFour, R., & Eaker, R. (1998). *Professional learning communities at work: Best practices for enhancing student achievement.* Alexandria, VA: Association for Supervision and Curriculum Development.

> This book provides a rich historical context for understanding the context of schools as organizations and the difficulties confronting schools in terms of the development of learning communities. It includes a number of useful chapters on the roles and strategies that principals, teachers, parents, and professional developers can play in supporting such communities.

Gordon, P., & Maxey, S. (2000). *How to help beginning teachers succeed.* Alexandria, VA: Association for Supervision and Curriculum Development.

> The authors focus on helping beginning teachers succeed through a Beginning Teacher Assistance Program or BTAP. Following a discussion on the needs of new teachers as uncovered through research, they delineate the goals of a new teacher induction program. The process used in developing a team and its program is described. A mentoring program model is outlined, and a rationale is provided for all elements of the model. The authors also supply guidance for constructing a summative evaluation of the program.

Hirsh, S., & Sparks, D. (1997). *A new vision for staff development.* Alexandria, VA: Association for Supervision and Curriculum Development.

> This book examines the contemporary strategies that successful districts are using to improve instruction. Comparisons are made of old and new models of staff development and their successes. Effective staff development means targeting everyone who affects learning and the total organization through multiple forms of learning. Shaping staff development includes (a) results-driven education, (b) systems thinking, and (c) constructivism. The focus has shifted in recent years from fragmented efforts to comprehensive planning, from adult needs to student needs, from off-site training to job-embedded learning, and from generic skills to a combination that includes content-specific skills.

Standards-Based Curriculum and Assessment Design

The standards movement is no longer new. Virtually every state has generated standards for graduation and, in many cases, for student attainment at different stages of its K–12 curriculum. Many states have increased the legitimacy of their standards by accompanying them with various forms of assessment, many of them standardized tests and most aligned—to some degree—with the standards. Much attention has been focused on standards and tests, but unfortunately not enough attention has been directed at the development of exemplary standards-based curricula, excellent classroom materials, and appropriate forms of assessment. Most teachers are not provided the time to develop such materials, and most school districts are too busy simply enduring the transition from a credit-bearing to a standards-based attainment system to work on such matters, let alone to determine which parts of the current curriculum are essential and which are redundant or obsolete.

In an environment where the need to increase test scores exerts constant pressure, it is critical that schools and educators find mechanisms to orient school systems toward the value of teaching to the standards and toward the development of rigorous and thoughtful models of best practice. This is especially important when we consider the forces that make it difficult for teachers to decide what is best to teach, such as our irreversible and growing information explosion and the lack of a national curriculum that dictates what should be learned. At the same time, schools are influenced by textbook publishers who are removed from local schools.

Too often, educators are detached from the results of their teaching because they have had little to no voice in the key decisions leading to those results. They teach curricula they have not developed, use textbooks they did not necessarily select, use an externally imposed scope and sequence, and rely on assessments that are not usually sufficiently representative of the curriculum taught (DuFour & Eaker, 1998). In this context, it is imperative that schools provide teachers the time to develop and deepen the knowledge and skills they need to make informed and responsible decisions about what should be taught and about how such knowledge should be organized.

This chapter addresses the question: How do we operationalize a standards-based and learner-centered curriculum so that all teachers will understand what it entails? It shows how to approach "unpacking," selecting, and then incorporating state standards into exemplary curricula by using the skills of local experts, primarily teachers.

Through the careful analysis of three science curriculum units—primary, intermediate, and secondary—this chapter showcases the critical components of learner-centered, standards-rich curriculum and assessment (Martin-Kniep, 2000; Wiggins & McTighe, 1998). I decided to showcase three specific units rather than provide readers with a number of examples from different subjects and grade levels because I wanted to illustrate the design process in depth. I also wanted to show the elegance of same-subject, vertical (cross-grade level) articulation and the manner in which the same design elements appear in different grade levels. Other books do a better job of describing different design elements or the standards-based design process itself (see, e.g., Stiggins, 1994; Wiggins, 1998). The design components illustrated in the three units I will describe are

1. Essential and guiding questions that launch and sustain student inquiry throughout the learning experience; such questions are the cornerstone of several reform efforts, including the Coalition of Essential Schools

2. Standards and indicators from at least two content areas that legitimize the unit's purpose and space within the overall curriculum (Martin-Kniep, 2000; Marzano, Pickering, & McTighe, 1993); note that the learning standards referred to in each unit having to do with mastery in science or literacy are common in most states as well as in national standards

3. Integrated learning (Jacobs, 1997) and assessment opportunities that consider a range of developmental needs and interests and provide teachers with ongoing feedback about students' learning

4. Rigor and inquiry to support the need for students to see themselves as researchers as well as active learners immersed in the process of making meaning of new information (Newmann et al., 1995)

5. Authentic culminating assessments that provide a real audience and purpose for students' work (Newmann & Associates, 1996; Wiggins, 1998)

6. Reflective and evaluative opportunities that enhance strategic thinking and self-monitoring (Thorpe, 2000)

When teachers and administrators design and implement curricula with these components in mind, they can clearly articulate their selected content with appropriate instructional strategies and assessments, as will be seen in the following unit overviews.

Good curriculum is close to a work of art. It is unique and personal. These three units address significant science content as well as other features of standards-based design. Readers who are interested in this design process can use the same design elements to create units in all subjects and grades by using the design template in Appendix B.

Each of these units has now been taught in one or more public schools several times.

"Expertise" is a 16-week second-grade unit developed by Pat Lynch, an elementary school teacher in Manhasset Public Schools, a medium-sized suburban district in Long Island, New York.[1] Her unit focuses on the concept of scientific expertise, and more specifically on the question of whether students can showcase "expertise" without having it. The content is paleontology, and the culminating performance assessment is the opportunity to act as a teaching volunteer at the American Museum of Natural History for one day. Students develop the skills of observing, inferring, and drawing final conclusions while developing their own paleontological research. They also develop their literacy abilities of reading, writing, speaking, and listening. Their research fosters the developing of their interviewing, note-taking, technological, and organizational skills.

"Laws of Science" is a 7-week sixth-grade unit developed by Lisa J. Boerum, a middle school special education teacher in a very small school district, Sag Harbor Public Schools, Long Island, New York.[2] The unit is also centered on science. Students ponder the truth behind scientific laws as they immerse themselves in the study of an unknown substance and the use of that substance to design a spacecraft. Two essential questions constitute the organizing center of the unit: "Are all scientific laws true?" and "Are all truths laws?" Throughout the unit, students pose and test hypotheses, conduct scientific experiments with different types of matter, document their scientific explorations formally, and find creative ways of applying and demonstrating their increased understandings. The unit culminates in a science convention in which students consider school, community, regional, and national events related to laws, technology, and science.

"A Quiet Garden" is a 4-week, ninth-grade earth science unit developed by Elizabeth Bedell, a high school teacher in the William Floyd School District, a medium-sized school district in Long Island, New York.[3] In this unit, students ponder the question that is the unit's organizing center: "What is more constant than change?" Through a careful examination of weathering and the opportunity to design a garden pond for the school's courtyard, students are guided through an exploration of the earth and the universe as a dynamic system. In this unit, students engage in hypothesis testing and experimental design while solving a plausible and practical problem.

I will describe the first unit in great depth and use the intermediate and secondary unit descriptions to illustrate the common characteristics among the three units and the ways in which they support one another.

"Expertise," the second-grade unit, begins with a description of the culminating assessment: Students are invited to consider becoming a teaching volunteer in a museum. In this case, students had access to the American Museum of Natural History in New York, but other museums, exhibitions, or displays would do. The teacher poses the essential question "Can you create a good museum and not know?" and returns to the question at different points throughout the unit. Whereas the question appears to be rather awkward in its construction, second graders quickly understand that it forces them to decide how much knowledge is needed for someone to capture the most important aspects of any topic or to call oneself an expert in something.

Most of the units described below and in subsequent chapters took place over several weeks. On selected days, whole periods or blocks were devoted to the activity; on other days, only a portion of the elementary day or part of the period or block was required. The point here is that this was not the exclusive instruction every day, although on some days it was.

The first 2 weeks of the unit establish students' prior knowledge of key concepts. These include expertise, research, museums, teaching volunteers, and paleontology. Concepts are introduced or clarified as needed.

The next 4 weeks focus on teaching the research process, including library use, note-taking, and technological skills. The support of the library media specialist is enlisted for this phase of the project to help teach library skills and provide materials. Texts related to paleontology are avoided at this point, so the emphasis is on the development of new skills, not on learning new content until that is appropriate.

During Week 7, students learn interviewing skills, generate lists of questions to ask a visiting teaching volunteer, conduct the actual interview, and write follow-up thank-you letters.

In Week 8, the focus of the project shifts toward developing student knowledge. Time is provided for students to become immersed in paleontology without yet having to incorporate their new research and note-taking skills. Most students at this age love to learn about dinosaurs and related information. Students explore materials available in the classroom and school library. Several books are read aloud by the teacher both to introduce major concepts and to model the reading of nonfiction.

During Weeks 9 through 11, students conduct independent research and are expected to apply their note-taking, library, and technological skills. Students continue to build their knowledge base about dinosaurs and current theories and controversies in the field of paleontology.

Weeks 11 and 12 are spent having pairs of students design plans for the exhibits in the dinosaur halls of a natural history museum. Each pair decides upon an organizational framework and uses research data to support the design they create. Using a teacher-created rubric, the class then assesses one group's project and uses that experience to inform further museum design revisions. (Rubrics and overviews related to the science units appear later in this chapter.)

Having seen and used a teacher-designed rubric (as opposed to a commercial one) to assess students' understanding in Week 12, students are now asked, in Week 13, to help the teacher design a rubric that will inform the creation, rehearsal, and assessment of their teaching volunteer performance. The class is divided into teaching volunteer groups of three to five members. Next, students in these groups self-select their own areas of expertise from a list of 25 exhibits currently on display in the American Museum of Natural History. Students are responsible for writing and performing the oral presentations for each area of expertise they have selected. They use their accumulated research documentation and the rubric to assist them in this process.

During Weeks 14 and 15, teaching volunteer groups rehearse both their individual presentations and the fluency of the total group presentation. Members use the oral presentation rubrics to coach each other. Students study maps to learn the location of particular exhibits in the museum.

The final week involves the teaching volunteer performance in the Dinosaur Halls of the American Museum of Natural History. Prior permission was arranged with the museum for this 1-day project. Teaching volunteer groups receive an individual schedule to adhere to and are responsible for leading their tour group through Saurischian Hall, the Omithiscian Hall, and the Teddy Roosevelt Rotunda. Tour groups are made up of parents and interested museum visitors. Parents are given evaluation forms, based on the rubric criteria that students have used before, to complete following the performance. Thank-you letters are written to museum staff, and a dinosaur cookie and juice party completes the unit, at which time students self-evaluate their participation in the unit.

Over the course of 19 weeks, the unit addresses and formally assesses a broad range of New York State Mathematics, Science and Technology Standards at the elementary level, including Science Standards 4.1a and 4.3b and Informational Systems Standard 2.1c. It also addresses most of the performance indicators in three out of four Language Arts Standards.

Undoubtedly, "Expertise" provides students with rigorous and rich opportunities to experience the benefits of knowing something so well they can teach it. This, in and of itself, is significant. The unit addresses much more than the content of paleontology. In fact, through this 19-week experience, students acquire a wide variety of reading, writing, measuring, research, and study skills. When one considers that the students who experience this unit are 8 years old and that, by the unit's end, they truly are able to function as docents in a museum of natural history, it is impossible not to be awed by the unit's power.

"Laws of Science" is an interdisciplinary language arts, science, and technology middle school unit that integrates language arts and science standards by adapting the Gateway to Educational Materials Science (GEMS) unit entitled "Oobleck" for a highly heterogeneous group of sixth-grade students, including several special education students.

The unit is launched with students responding to the essential questions: "Are all scientific laws true?" and "Are all truths laws?" Students then read aloud *Bartholomew and the Oobleck* by Dr. Seuss. Next, they work in small groups on a lab investigation to determine the properties of an unknown substance made of cornstarch, water, and food coloring. They use all their senses except taste in order to determine its properties. After the students individually chart their observations, the groups work to develop a hypothesis about the substance. They perform miniexperiments to prove or disprove their hypothesis about the substance.

After the experiments are completed, students participate in a science convention to determine the truth about the substance and to state it as precisely as they can using scientific terms. The groups come together to listen to their peers' experimental results and to critically discuss them. The goal is to determine the "laws" of the substance. As the groups share the properties they discovered during the lab investigation, the class determines if each property is true and valid or if there are any situations during which the property would not be true. Students resolve disagreements by adding phrases, defining terms, or experimenting further to arrive at the truth.

In the next segment of this unit, students apply their knowledge and understanding about the properties of the unknown substance as they design a spacecraft that is able to successfully land on and take off manually from an ocean of the substance. Students work in their groups to design a plan considering the substance's properties. Using available materials and their own imaginations, they construct a model based on their design plans.

The final project involves having students work individually or in a group to develop a performance project that creatively addresses the answers to the essential questions. They use prior knowledge from previous science units and research various scientific laws. Finally, they address selected school, community, regional, or national current events related to laws, technology, and science.

In "Laws of Science," students question the meaning and value of truths and laws by experiencing and experimenting with them. The artistry of the unit lies in its careful attention to the inquiry process, as is evident by some of the questions that students address. These questions include:

- What process did we go through to arrive at the "laws" of the substance?
- What was easy or difficult in determining the "laws" of the substance?
- In what ways are we scientists?
- What have you learned from your peers through this convention?
- In what ways did your group work and communicate effectively?
- Explain the process you went through to design your spacecraft.

- Explain the difficulties you experienced *and* how you overcame them.
- Explain what other features could have gone into your design *and* why your chosen design is optimal for a successful landing and take-off.
- In what ways does technology help us to arrive at truths?

This unit succeeds in enabling students to acquire essential inquiry and communication skills. It also enables them to integrate literature, science, and technology in natural and meaningful ways. Among the state standards and performance indicators that are formally assessed are the following New York State Mathematics, Science and Technology Standards at the intermediate level: Standards 1a, b, c, d, e, f, h, and i; Standard 4b; and Standards 5a, b, c, d, and e. The unit also assesses numerous performance indicators in all four New York State English Language Arts standards.

In "The Quiet Garden," a ninth-grade earth science unit, students are asked to design a garden pond for a school courtyard. In the design procedure, they specifically assess the suitability of common rocks as decorative materials around the pond. The focus is to have students gain confidence in using the scientific method by creating hypotheses, predictions, and tests that they then analyze, allowing them to modify the hypotheses and ponder new questions that arise.

The unit begins with an essential question, one that runs through the entire earth science curriculum: "What is more constant than change?" Students are expected to view the earth and the universe as a dynamic system after studying earth processes.

Students then consider the question "What causes rocks at the earth's surface to change?" The discussion flows into the concept of weathering and the agents that bring it about. To put a practical and proximal twist to the concepts, students are directed to design a garden pond for a nearby courtyard, using the scientific method to determine which commonly available rock materials would be suitable as coping stones and decorations.

The unit includes opportunities for students to work as a whole class, in small groups, and individually. Many activities begin in the large-group or collaborative setting (brainstorming, class discussions, and developing hypotheses), move to a smaller lab group for further investigation (designing experimental procedures and carrying out experiments), and end as individuals use the new knowledge to produce lab reports, a garden plan, and journal responses. Often class discussion of an individual's work leads to a new cycle of investigation.

As with the preceding units, inquiry is central. The unit's craft lies in the application of scientific content to the solution of a problem. The unit formally assesses seven performance indicators in Standard 1, three performance indicators in Standard 4, and three performance indicators in Standard 7 of the New York State Mathematics, Science and Technology Standards. The unit also evaluates students on two of the four English Language Arts Standards.

All three of these units are centered on science and scientific inquiry, each with its unique angle or organizing center. Individually, they are all strong curriculum units that embody well-crafted design decisions. For example, each of them shows a strategic focus on specific standards. Tables 2.1, 2.2, and 2.3 show partial sketches of each unit (a portion of the schedule of activities and assessments and the standards addressed).

Though each teacher will have a unique style in showing the relationships among learning opportunities, assessments, and standards, all three unit sketches explicitly show the relationships among these three components. Furthermore, in all three cases, the three teachers who first did the projects cite standards and performance indicators that are

Table 2.1 Partial Sketch of the Unit "Expertise"

Week	Monday	Tuesday	Wednesday	Thursday	Friday
4	**Teach Research and Note-Taking Skills**				
Activities	Library Media Center Introduce computer programs available for research: • Golden Books • World Book Mini-lessons: • Captions • Pronunciation	Library Media Center Introduce computer programs • Grollier's *Prehistoric Encyclopedia* Mini-lesson: • Captions	Library Media Center Introduce the Internet • Netscape • Bookmarks	Library Media Center Teach note taking • Paraphrasing • Selecting important facts	Library Media Center Teach note taking • Shortcuts • Use of phrases • Abbreviations
Assessments (pages cited are those of prototype)	Journal entry, p. 14			Journal entry, p. 14	Journal entry, p. 15
Standards	ELa1–1a, 1b, 1d MST2–Info. Sys. 1C	ELa1–1b, 1d MST2–Info. Sys. 1C	ELa1–1b, 1d MST2–Info. Sys. 1C	ELa1–1b, 1c	ELa1–1c
5	**Teach Research and Note-Taking Skills**				
Activities	Mini-lessons: • Topic • Main ideas	Mini-lessons: • Highlighting	Mini-lessons: • Charts, maps, and captions • Skimming for specific information • Relevant information • Irrelevant information	Mini-lessons: • Classification • Highlighting	
Assessments	Journal entry, p. 15	Cloze exercise—How to Do Research, pp. 47–48	Journal entry, p. 15	Journal entry, p. 15	
Standards	ELa1–1a, 1c	ELa1–1c	ELa1–1a, 1b	ELa1–1c	
6	**Teach Research and Note-Taking Skills**				
Activities	Mini-lesson: • Finding related topics and headings	Mini-lesson: • Organizing research	Mini-lesson: • Setting up research file box		
Assessments					
Standards	ELa1–1b	ELa–1c	ELa1–1c		

Table 2.2   Partial Sketch of the Unit "Laws of Science"

Week 5: Monday	Tuesday	Wednesday	Thursday	Friday
Module 6	**Module 6**	**Module 7**	**Module 7**	**Module 7**
Scientific Convention	*Scientific Convention*	*Spacecraft Design: Plan and Design*	*Spacecraft Design: Construct and Test*	*Spacecraft Design: Test and Reflect*
The students will participate in a scientific convention to determine the truth about Oobleck and to state it as clearly and completely as possible.	The students will participate in a scientific convention to determine the truth about Oobleck and to state it as clearly and completely as possible.	The students will apply their knowledge and understanding about the properties of Oobleck in order to design a spacecraft that would be able to successfully land on and take off from an ocean of Oobleck.	The students will apply their knowledge and understanding about the properties of Oobleck in order to design a spacecraft that would be able to successfully land on and take off from an ocean of Oobleck.	The students will apply their knowledge and understanding about the properties of Oobleck in order to design a spacecraft that would be able to successfully land on and take off from an ocean of Oobleck.
Summative Assessment	*Summative Assessment*	*Formative Assessment*	*Formative Assessment*	*Summative Assessment*
Participation in scientific convention, pp. 62–68	Participation in scientific convention, pp. 62–68 Rubric for scientific convention, p. 61 Responses to reflection questions, p. 69	Plans for spacecraft design, p. 76 Rubric for spacecraft design, p. 77	Plans for spacecraft design, p. 76 Rubric for spacecraft design, p. 77	Responses to reflection questions, pp. 78, 80–81 Spacecraft model reflection prompt Rubric for spacecraft design, p. 77
Indicators: (See Overview) MST 1h ELA 1b ELA 3a ELA 4a, b	**Indicators:** (See Overview) MST 1h ELA 1b ELA 3a ELA 4a, b	**Indicators:** (See Overview) MST 5a, b, c, d, e	**Indicators:** (See Overview) MST 5a, b, c, d, e	**Indicators:** (See Overview) MST 5a, b, c, d, e

Note: Page numbers referred to in the assessments are those of the published prototype.

addressed by the unit's assessments and not the ones that are present in the lessons themselves. The reason for this bias is that true evidence of standards attainment is found in what students, not the teacher, can do.

Given the significant and explicit attention to standards, these units, in fact, prepare students to meet the demands of state tests without reducing the integrity of the science curriculum. This is illustrated by the three boxes of sample items starting on page 24, typical of the intermediate-level science assessment administered in New York State at the eighth-grade level.

All three units use essential and guiding questions as learning and assessment opportunities. Teachers use these questions as diagnostic and summative assessment by asking students to ponder them at the beginning and end of each unit and, in some cases, to

Table 2.3   Partial Sketch of the Unit "A Quiet Garden"

	Module Plan
Module 4	A Practical Application of the Scientific Method: Studying the Factors That Affect the Type and Rate of Weathering
Learning opportunities	The Scientific Method ➤ Review the scientific method and develop rubric for a good experiment; use an example to go through the steps of the scientific method. ➤ As a group, students observe weathered rocks and develop the hypothesis: *"Rocks weather when they are exposed to the atmosphere, hydrosphere, and biosphere."* ➤ As a class or in lab groups, make predictions, and have students design experiments to investigate the factors that affect the type and rate of weathering (surface area, mineral composition, temperature, duration of weathering, etc.). An example: *"If rocks weather by exposure to the hydrosphere, then the exterior of rocks will be more weathered that the interiors."* ➤ Carry out experiments, gather data, devise report sheets, create graphic presentations, write lab reports. Reflection ➤ Use rubric to evaluate their experiments. ➤ Seek connections between their experiments and the garden design. ➤ Class discussion: "What have we learned?" Share results and problems and formulate new questions.
Assessments	Experiment designs (predictions, materials lists, procedures) Report sheet and graph layouts Observations recorded on report sheets with graphs of data Written report Reflection
New York State standards/outcomes	MST 1, 4 ELA 1, 3, CDOS 3a, Reflection
Elements of the Earth Science Program modification curriculum addressed	Unit 4: A1, 2, 4, 5 (in addition, there is an opportunity at this time to review Unit 2: Rocks and Minerals)

self-assess the changes between the two using explicitly stated criteria in the form of a checklist or rubric.

Boxes 2.4 and 2.5 are pre- and post-test answers to the essential question from a ninth-grade student in Elizabeth Bedell's class who was also a third-time repeater of ninth grade.

The changes between the pretest and the posttest are significant. The pretest is composed of two generalizations with no support. The posttest response incorporates different aspects of the unit's contents. Furthermore, the student uses specific factual evidence to support the assertion that change is the only constant thing.

Teachers use the guiding questions to grapple with the unit's components. The questions also guide students' research and work toward a culminating authentic task.

The three units also consider the diverse ability and developmental needs of students by relying on learning experiences that cater to different learning styles and intelligences and by enabling students to make choices of either content or ways of representing it. In "Expertise," the choice revolves around a specific aspect of paleontology. In "Laws of Science," students can choose both the events they will address and the means for showing

Box 2.1   Item 1: Rock Cycle

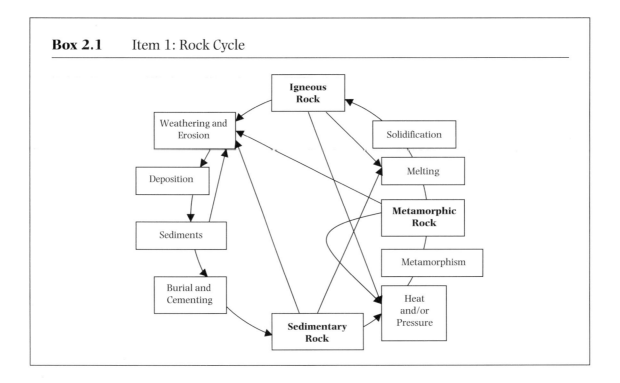

Box 2.2   Item 2

A student plays tennis several times a week. She notices that the tennis ball seems to bounce higher on some courts than on other courts. She wonders if this has something to do with the surface of the court. Design an experiment to see if her hypothesis is correct. Include these elements in your response:

- State the hypothesis
- Identify the factor to be varied
- Identify two factors that should be held constant
- Clearly describe the procedures

Box 2.3   Item 3

For each question, write your answer in the space provided on the separate answer sheet.

Base your answers to Questions 35 and 36 on the charts below, which show two elements (iron and sulfur) and their properties. The arrows indicate that these elements may combine to form either a mixture of iron and sulfur or the compound iron sulfide.

Question 35. How could a student use a magnet to indicate that combining iron and sulfur to produce the mixture of iron and sulfur is a physical change?

Question 36. What evidence indicates that a chemical change took place when the iron and sulfur combined to form iron sulfide?

Box 2.4

What is more constant than change?

"Nothing Change happens everyday all day to everybody from light to dark, the time of day or everyday life as to your daily routine. Change is happening all the time which makes it the most common thing." *(Pretest, February 2)*

Box 2.5

"The only thing constant is change.

I know change is constant because of weathering that takes place and erosion. An example of the weathering and erosion is how much the beach has changed. Because of the weathering such as the wind, and storms. The beach has changed totally it was eroded and there is no more beach there. Streams also change all the time a stream can go from a young stream to a mature stream and then to an old stream. You know this be seeing how the stream gets steeper and wider. Glaciers are also another part of change. Glaciers are formed by more snow falling then melting. The glaciers can get bigger or smaller depending on the weatherthey are constantly changing. Rocks can also change constantly from weathering. The size and shape of a rock can change because of the weathering that occurs to it. The wind abrasion changes the shapes of rocks and erodes them. They change into new shapes." *(Post-test, March 23)*

---

how these events relate to truth, laws, technology, and science. In "A Quiet Garden," choice lies in students' having to devise experiments and strategies for designing an attractive, non-toxic, and durable pond with a solar pump, a plastic pond liner, and a budget of $150.

In all of these units, students are able to articulate their thinking and learning process and to evaluate their own and each other's learning. They are also able to use different learning modalities and, in some cases, their preferred intelligence to demonstrate the learning attained as a result of the unit. All of these unit attributes are indicative of effective teaching practices, which, in turn, correlate positively with student achievement (Stronge, 2002). In "Expertise," students keep a journal of their learning. Box 2.6 is a sample unedited entry.

In "Laws of Science," students record their thoughts as they formulate hypotheses such as the ones shown in Boxes 2.4 and 2.5.

Model Format: IF (my action) **THEN** (substance's reaction).

Student Samples:

1. **If** I hold it in my hand, **then** it will melt because of body heat.

2. **If** I poke it, **then** it will feel thick.

3. **If** I touch it, **then** it will stick to me.

Box 2.6

"Yesterday we went to the high school and in the board room and we each had to do speeches for their slides. The people who did it where: James, Jamie, Allison C., John, Peter, Megan La., and I. The six people and I had about 4, 5, or 5 speeches. We did it in front of an adeance and the board of Ed! Our parents wher part of the adeance. We wher osaum! We are practacly too famous for second graders!!"

---

4. **If** I tilt the bowl, **then** the substance will make a wave.

5. **If** I squeeze it, **then** the liquid substance will come out.

6. **If** I put the substance on paper, **then** it will dry.

7. **If** I add water to the substance, **then** it will drip.

8. **If** I pick up the substance, **then** it will crumble.

9. **If** I keep the substance on my hand, **then** it will dry.

Students also respond to reflective questions such as the following ones:

- How well do your procedures and observations relate to your hypothesis?
- Was your hypothesis proven to be true? Why or why not?
- From your experiment only, do you have evidence to support that the substance is a SOLID? a LIQUID? a GAS? Pick one and explain why.

In "A Quiet Garden," students respond to reflective questions throughout their inquiry. Such inquiry questions include:

- What have you learned from your experiments that you can apply to the pond design?
- What questions do you have about the materials? (Remember, there will be a fountain with running water in the garden.)
- How realistic were your experiments? (Did they simulate the actual conditions?) Is it important that the experiments simulate the garden conditions?

All three units include explicit performance criteria embodied in checklists and rubrics that students use to assess and monitor the quality of their work. These criteria are directly related to the state and national standards that support the units and in fact often "lift" that language directly from these standards. Tables 2.4, 2.5, and 2.6 include sample rubrics.

As a set, these units illustrate the beauty of a spiral curriculum that is respectful of students' changing needs and understandings. One can easily imagine that the knowledge and skills acquired in "Expertise" would enable students to maximize their learning from "Laws of Science" and that the latter would greatly enhance students' work in "A Quiet Garden."

Table 2.4   Partial Rubric From "Expertise"

Rubric for Teaching Volunteer Performance

Criteria: Oral Presentation Skills

	Superior	*Good*	*Satisfactory*	*Needs Improvement*
Volume and intensity	Constantly anticipates and adjusts for external conditions and the size of the space and audience. Volume, intensity, and speaking locution are adjusted accordingly so that museum visitors can hear well.	Volume and intensity are appropriate for the area and conditions. Adjusts to changes as they become apparent. Museum visitors hear well most of the time.	Volume and intensity tend to stay constant at a satisfactory level. Doesn't monitor and adjust sufficiently to changing conditions. Some museum visitors may not hear as conditions alter.	Volume and intensity too loud or soft for the area and conditions. No monitoring and adjusting to conditions. Distracting volume and intensity for museum visitors. Interferes with delivery of information.
Articulation	Highly articulate. Speaks clearly and distinctly. Careful enunciation. Lively expression. Speaking is easily perceptible to museum visitors, and its expressive quality enhances the power of the speaking.	Vocal expression is clear and distinct. Museum visitors can hear and understand the Teaching Volunteer's spoken words.	Vocal expression clear at times and indistinct at other times. Museum visitors occasionally have difficulty hearing and understanding the Teaching Volunteer's spoken words.	Speaking is indistinct. May mumble and/or slur words. Careless enunciation. Museum visitor unable to understand the speaking.
Pace of delivery	Consistently appropriate for museum visitors to take in the material. Neither too fast nor too slow. Adjusts pace to meet visitors' needs. Presentation is completed on time, and the pace is steady throughout.	Steady pace that is neither too fast nor too slow. Some adjustments are needed to accomplish an on-time completion. Adjustments don't interfere with museum visitors' experience.	Pace inconsistent. At times too fast and/or too slow. Museum visitors feel rushed at times or feel that the presentation drags at others. Tour finishes close to the allotted time.	Pace is too fast and/or too slow. Tour finishes too early or too late.
Physical presentation	Maintains an engaging yet calm, poised, professional demeanor at all times and under all circumstances. Appropriate eye contact is maintained throughout. All gestures and motions are appropriate and enhance the speaking and the audience's comfort level and participation. Body positioning doesn't block visitors' view of exhibits.	Appears comfortable in role. Posture, motions, and body language appropriate. Does not stand so as to block view of exhibits.	Posture, motions, and body language are distracting at times. Sometimes appears anxious and/or uninterested and appears comfortable at other times. Eye contact mostly appropriate; at times may avoid eye contact and/or stare inappropriately. Body position at times blocks museum visitors' view of exhibits.	Body language suggests anxiety and/or lack of interest. Appears uncomfortable with the role. Motions, gestures, and body language are distracting for museum visitors. Stands so as to interfere with view of exhibits.

Table 2.5   Partial Rubric From "Laws of Science"

Science/Language Arts:

Date:

Dimensions	Novice	Apprentice	Practitioner	Expert
Observations/ results – Organization – Relevance – Supporting details	Observations are presented but are difficult to understand. Observations/ results need to relate to hypothesis with evidence of observable facts. Observations/ results need to have details that clarify the observations and support the procedures, materials, and hypothesis.	Observations are evident but need to be presented in a chart or diagram for clarity and organization. Observations/ results are indirectly related to the hypothesis with facts that need to be stated clearly. Observations/ results have details, but the details need to be explained further to more fully support the procedures, materials, and hypothesis.	Observations are clear and organized. Observations/ results relate to hypothesis. Observations/ results contain details that support the procedures, materials, and hypothesis.	Observations are presented in a clear, organized, identifiable manner, using charts, diagrams, or paragraphs. Observations give evidence of observable facts that strongly relate to the hypothesis. Observations/ results contain a variety of details that support the appropriateness of the procedures, materials, and hypothesis.
Conclusion – Understanding – Use of data – Supporting details	An ending thought has been written, but it needs to communicate what has been learned about how procedures and observations prove or disprove the hypothesis. Conclusions are drawn, but the relationship to the data is not clear. Explanations need to be written and supported with relevant details.	Communicates what has been learned, but thoughts need to relate to how the procedures and observations prove or disprove hypothesis. Conclusions are supported by data but need to be explained. Details are limited and need to be relevant to the procedure and hypothesis.	Communicates what has been learned about how procedures and observations prove or disprove the hypothesis. Conclusions are supported, but the scope of the conclusions is broader than what the data support. Relevant details help support part of the conclusions.	Communicates what has been learned about how procedures and observations prove or disprove the hypothesis with a significant level of insight. Conclusions are supported by data with explanations, and all data are accounted for. Explanations are supported with a variety of relevant detail.

Table 2.6 Partial Rubric From "A Quiet Garden"

Teacher-Designed Rubric for Scientific Experiments

	Researcher	Research Assistant	Laboratory Assistant	Lab Assistant-in-Training
Data collection and analysis (the degree to which the observations are made and analyzed with care)	Observations are thorough and relevant; measurements are accurate, with all appropriate units included Data are complete and organized, with all units identified Correctly applies mathematical concepts, correctly displays calculations (formula, substitution, and answer) with an explanation of how and why the calculation was done Graphs and charts are labeled and titled; visual representations are referred to in text; dependent and independent variables are appropriately situated on graph; key is clearly labeled	Observations are relevant; measurements are accurate, with most appropriate units included Data are complete and organized, with most units identified Correctly applies mathematical concepts, correctly displays calculations (formula, substitution, and answer) Graphs and charts are labeled and titled; dependent and independent variables are appropriately situated on graph; units and/or key is missing	Observations and measurements contain consistent errors Data are complete, but organization makes it difficult to follow; units are missing, incomplete, or incorrect Correctly applies mathematical concepts; calculation is complete but work is not shown; units may be missing Graphs and charts are incomplete; dependent and independent variables are reversed on graph; units, labels, and/or titles are missing	Observations and measurements are incomplete or contain large errors Data are complete, but organization makes it difficult to follow; units are missing, incomplete, or incorrect Omits calculations or incorrectly applies mathematical concepts Lacks visual representations (graphs or charts)

WHAT DOES IT TAKE TO DEVELOP A STANDARDS-BASED, LEARNER-CENTERED UNIT?

The three units described in this chapter were written by teachers who made a significant commitment to learn about standards-based design, to incorporate it into their classroom practice, and to document it in a way that would allow other teachers to understand and follow all their curriculum and assessment decisions. Such commitment, in the form of 5 release days during the school year and 1 week in the summer in 3 consecutive years, was supported by their principals and district superintendents. In that period of time, teachers designed the preceding units but also drafted and refined several more. They also became local curriculum and assessment resource providers for other teachers in their schools and facilitated the design and implementation of units for grades K–12.

There are other ways of involving teachers in standards-based curricula. Among these are engaging them in a gap analysis of the operational curriculum (asking them to map their lessons and units against local and state standards and then make adjustments and revisions to their curriculum to better address underemphasized standards) or in a gap analysis of the learned curriculum (asking them to assess the distance between what they believe are standards-based lessons and assignments and resulting student work from students representing a range of academic attainment). My experience is that while these processes are extremely worthwhile, designing a complete standards-based unit provides teachers with a deeper understanding of the standards vis-à-vis the curriculum than any other curriculum-related process. Furthermore, designing a unit for an audience other than oneself results in a deeper understanding of the relationship among the different components of standards-based and learner-centered design. This, in turn, results in the development of teachers' capacity to help other teachers design.

The teachers who developed these units needed a forum that embraced curriculum development and that supported collaborative work. Each draft of the template was reviewed and analyzed by other teachers involved in curriculum design, as well as by local and outside content and curriculum experts. This extended community validated teachers' efforts and provided the motivation to produce high-quality work.

HOW DO WE HELP TEACHERS DEVELOP HIGH-QUALITY STANDARDS-BASED UNITS?

Teachers need significant background in standards-based design and learner-centered education. This background is acquired over time, and it is critical that staff developers and administrators give teachers many opportunities to review the standards and create units that support them. The translation of local, state, or national standards into teachers' own words; the identification of content, skills, activities, strategies, and assessments that teachers use to address specific standards and indicators; and the rating of the extent to which teachers' curricula introduce, reinforce, or seek mastery of specific performance indicators are all strategies for helping teachers unpack and internalize the standards.

To support the design process, teachers can benefit from design templates and frameworks. The teachers who wrote these units used the design template included in Appendix B. This template uses a backwards or outcome-based process such as the one found in Marzano et al. (1993) or Wiggins and McTighe (1998).

In this template, teachers begin the process by identifying an organizing center around which the unit will be designed. Ideally, this organizing center is generative, enabling teachers to address a concept, issue, or problem in depth while making meaningful interdisciplinary connections as well as connections between the learner and the material taught. Next, teachers consider the outcomes and standards they want students to attain at the end of the unit. They then operationalize these outcomes and standards by addressing the questions:

- What does each outcome/standard look like?
- What does each mean in my classroom/subject/grade?
- What will students produce if they are working to attain the outcomes/standards?

Teachers then identify the assessments they need to collect or administer before (diagnostic), during (formative), and after (summative) the unit is completed to demonstrate that students have grown toward and/or achieved desired standards or outcomes. As part of the assessment considerations, teachers ponder the questions:

- How will I communicate what mastery or accomplishment means?
- What does quality mean for me and my students?
- How good is good enough?

Once teachers have addressed issues related to assessment and performance criteria, they shift their attention to the unit as experienced by the learners. They ponder the possible use of essential and guiding questions to harness students' interest and motivation and to focus their teaching. They also identify or design the learning opportunities they need to provide so that different kinds of students can attain desired learning outcomes and standards.

It is not easy to design a unit like the ones previously described, but this is what is required if the state and national standards are going to be attained and if we want to increase a school's capacity to design, assess, or adapt quality curricula to enhance student learning. Ideally, schools must find time for teachers to come together for periods of 7 to 20 days over a year or two, depending on the complexity of the unit, to determine the standards that are addressed and are missing by their current curriculum materials, to design performance and authentic assessment measures that incorporate desired standards, to collect materials, and to create rubrics and other tasks. A unit draft undergoes significant change during the implementation phase and often gets transformed every time it is taught. Teachers need shorter meetings after a unit is taught to review what happened and make revisions to increase its effectiveness. Staff developers can play a critical role in supporting this process by reviewing and responding to teachers' work on a continuous basis.

We all live in the real world of schools and understand that every teacher cannot be granted one or more weeks of design time each year; however, schools must provide some time for small groups of teachers to have time each year for this effort, or the standards will have no meaning in students' lives. Once units are created, other teachers at a grade level can use them as they are or with very minor modifications. Staff developers and administrators can provide the structures for such use and adaptations.

Providing teachers with a collaborative forum for the development of curricula where teachers help each other design, review, and revise their work is likely to raise the bar for each teacher's unit design, as well as to facilitate the creation of collegial structures within the school.

Despite the demands of time and energy, the investment in standards-based design is worth it. Data from a variety of studies provide evidence that teaching experience is the single most important factor in enhancing student learning (Wright et al., 1997) and that it results in an up to 30% increase in students' academic performance (Stronge, 2002).

When teachers experience and practice this standards-based design process, they accomplish far more than the design of a unit. The process of articulating all the design components into a whole unified by an organizing center forces teachers to ask themselves critical questions about all the content they teach and not just about the content of the unit they are designing.

Furthermore, when teachers implement the unit they have designed, experience the benefits of ongoing assessment, feel the power of authentic culminating experiences, and recognize the value of ascertaining students' thinking processes as they unfold, they internalize the value of these learner-centered practices and embed them in their day-to-day practice. As increasingly effective teachers, they serve as powerful examples of lifelong learners for their colleagues and for their own students.

POSSIBLE QUESTIONS FOR THE READER

1. Who develops the curriculum in your school or district? When is that curriculum developed? How is it developed?

2. What standards of quality, if any, guide the curriculum development process in your school or district? Who enacts those standards?

3. What role do administrators and staff developers play in the curriculum design or revision process?

4. What are the expectations related to who uses the curriculum that is developed and how the curriculum is used?

5. How are teachers supported in the internalization and use of national or state standards?

6. How are the design and implementation of curriculum and assessment processes that meet quality standards supported in your school or school district?

7. What processes exist to ensure that students learn national or state standards?

RECOMMENDED BOOKS ON STANDARDS-BASED CURRICULUM AND ASSESSMENT DESIGN

Burke, K. (Ed.). (1996). *Authentic assessment: A collection.* Palatine, IL: IRI/Skylight.
This collection succinctly dispels the myth that *authentic assessment* is merely the latest buzzword. It traces the history of National Assessment of Educational Progress (NAEP) trends, competency testing, and influences of the National Governors Association upon authentic instruction. It then defines, explains, and provides examples of authentic, alternative assessments. Many secondary school examples are included. In addition, each section includes an extensive bibliography of related articles.

Drake, S. (1998). *Creating integrated curriculum.* Thousand Oaks, CA: Sage.
This book offers elementary, middle, and high school educators an extensive look at different approaches to curriculum integration. It provides a rationale for integrating the curriculum and includes models to assist in understanding various approaches. Sample lessons, units, and planning strategies help the reader understand and employ the basic concepts of interdisciplinary, thematic, and problem-based approaches to learning. Drake dispels the notion that effective curriculum integration is "business as usual." It is rather a critical part of educational reform involving curriculum, standards, assessments, and instructional strategies.

Ellis, A. K., & Stuen, C. J. (1998). *The interdisciplinary curriculum.* Raleigh, NC: Eye on Education.
This book includes chapters on the nature of knowledge, the components of the inquiry process, concept formation, and reflective thinking. It also addresses issues such as

integration of subject matter and academic integrity, the importance of major themes, and the role of experience in learning. The authors offer classroom-tested examples and models of interdisciplinary curricula at different grade levels and involving different subjects.

Hart, D. (1994). *Authentic assessment: A handbook for educators.* New York: Addison-Wesley.

This book is an excellent assessment primer. It provides readers with a basic understanding and knowledge of assessment and related issues. Each chapter contains definitions of pertinent terms and provides many examples in chart or graph form. The book also includes an extensive assessment glossary and a bibliography of supporting resources in assessment. The topics covered by this book include standardized testing as compared to authentic assessment; portfolio assessment; performance assessment; and scoring and grading strategies.

Hill, C., & Norwick, L. (1998). *Classroom based assessment.* Norwood, MA: Christopher-Gordon.

This book is the first of four in a new series on assessment. It presents practical ways to collect information about young learners. It addresses teacher notebooks, an observing-as-assessment continuum, assessment forms, and recommended readings. It emphasizes assessments in reading and writing, but other content areas are also addressed.

Jacobs, H. H. (1997). *Mapping the big picture: Integrating curriculum and assessment K–12.* Alexandria, VA: Association for Supervision and Curriculum Development.

In this book, Jacobs writes about curriculum mapping, particularly as a procedure for collecting data about a school district's curricula by using the school calendar as an organizer. The school calendar serves as the framework for this procedure. Jacobs goes on to explain that curriculum mapping increases the possibilities for short- and long-term planning and clear communication among educators. Curriculum maps allow teachers to find repetitions, gaps, meaningful assessments, potential areas of integration, and areas needing work. Jacobs also devotes a chapter to the definition and importance of essential questions.

Kuhn, T. (1992). *Mathematics assessment: Alternative approaches.* Columbia, SC: National Council of Teachers of Mathematics.

This video and viewer guide focus on alternative assessment in mathematics. The video is broken up into six segments, which cover the introduction and implementation of alternative assessment in the mathematics classroom. Each video segment has two parts, classroom and faculty interactions and panel discussions. The guide provides video summaries and extended activities for staff development. This is a good tool that staff developers can use to introduce alternative assessment in mathematics.

McCollum, S. L. (1994). *Performance assessment in the social studies classroom: A how-to book for teachers.* Joplin, MO: Chalk Dust.

This book explores authentic social studies performance assessments in Grades 4 through 12. Each of the 14 individual tasks is directly tied to social studies concepts, content, and skills and is related to real-world experiences. The author (a social studies teacher) gives the reader clearly outlined task instructions, materials, Blackline Masters, task-specific rubrics, student checklists, and examples of students' work.

Miller, B., & Singleton, L. (1995). *Preparing citizens: Linking authentic assessment and instruction in civic/law-related education.* Boulder, CO: Social Science Education Consortium.

This book makes critical connections between civic education curriculum, instruction, and assessment. Among its strengths are (a) a collection of authentic tasks supported by assessment procedures; (b) a strong emphasis on the use of rubrics in classroom instruction, including clear step-by-step instructions for development and revision; and (c) samples, methods, and suggestions in classroom instruction that are grounded by presentation through personal experiences and case studies of teachers who have used them. The teacher reflections and revisions are also especially helpful in providing insight into the design of tasks.

Newmann, F. W., Secada, W. G., & Wehlage, G. G. (1995). *A guide to authentic instruction and assessment: Vision, standards and scoring.* Madison: Wisconsin Center for Education Research.

This book identifies three criteria for authentic learning tasks: the construction of knowledge, disciplined inquiry, and value beyond school. The authors discuss these criteria as they relate to tasks, instruction, and student performance and further break the three criteria down into standards. Examples from mathematics and social studies are provided for each of the standards identified. These examples cross grade levels. Finally, the text provides scoring criteria for judging the authenticity of assessment tasks, instruction, and student performance.

Stiggins, R. J. (1994). *Student-centered classroom assessment.* New York: Merrill.

This book focuses on ways to develop and use sound classroom assessments and on strategies to involve students as partners in the assessment process. It presents a balanced look at all kinds of assessments. It includes a variety of classroom applications; discusses ways to communicate student achievement, including report cards versus portfolios; and provides a reflection section that could be used in staff development activities.

Wiggins, G. (1998). *Educative assessment: Designing assessments to inform and improve student performance.* San Francisco: Jossey-Bass.

This book is aimed at enabling educators to create assessments that will improve performance and not merely audit it. It calls for the use of authentic tasks, feedback methods for teacher and students while learning is in progress, and resulting adjustments during the entire process. It is replete with charts, graphs, examples, and diagrams that make it both readable and practical. The models provided can actually be altered and used in the classroom without much work. Standards and criteria are explained and samples of rubrics included. The rubric construction is thoroughly demonstrated. The intricacies of portfolio assessment are also explored, and sample charts for inclusion and evaluation are provided.

Wiggins, G., & McTighe, J. (1998). *Understanding by design.* Alexandria, VA: Association for Supervision and Curriculum Development.

Teachers would agree that, whatever the content, their goal is that students will understand a concept or process. But what is understanding? The authors explain six facets of understanding. They propose a "backward design" model: after determining what students need to know and be able to do, teachers should design the assessments that show evidence of this understanding. Readers are carefully taken through this design process, with classroom examples as well as design templates. Issues of constructivism, conceptual change, and strategies for deciding the content that does not need to be taught naturally arise in the discussion. Though primarily useful to the classroom teacher, this book should be of considerable interest to any professional involved in curriculum design.

NOTES

1. Pat Lynch, "Expertise," 1999, a Standards-Based Curriculum and Assessment Prototype available from the Center for the Study of Expertise in Teaching and Learning (CSETL) Web site, *www.csetl.org/curriculum_units.htm.*

2. Lisa J. Boerum, "Laws of Science," 1999, a Standards-Based Curriculum and Assessment Prototype available from the Center for the Study of Expertise in Teaching and Learning (CSETL) Web site, *www.csetl.org/curriculum_units.htm.*

3. Elizabeth Bedell, "A Quiet Garden," 2000, a Standards-Based Curriculum and Assessment Prototype available from the Center for the Study of Expertise in Teaching and Learning (CSETL) Web site, *www.csetl.org/curriculum_units.htm.*

Data-Driven Inquiry and Action Research

Data-driven inquiry and action research are critical aspects in the development of the professional identity of individual teachers and learning communities (Bernhardt, 1998; Kouzes & Posner, 1999; Noffke & Stevenson, 1995). They both involve asking questions and identifying problems that can be solved by using data. This chapter addresses the question: How do we enable teachers to pursue questions of great significance about their practice? It explores three approaches to inquiry: individual, collaborative, and schoolwide. One is not more important than the others, but together they foster a culture that values and uses data to diagnose, monitor, and ultimately improve teaching and learning.

All inquiry begins with a question to be answered or a problem to be solved. When individual educators pursue an action research question, the expected answer results in changes or improvements within the immediate context of the individual's work (the classroom or students for the teacher; work with specific adults for administrators). When groups of educators pursue a question, their contexts expand, and so does their resulting impact. Finally, when entire schools pursue a common question, the school develops a collective identity. Though scope of impact and involvement may be considered the most important criteria for emphasizing collaborative research over individual inquiry, the nature of the question asked and the depth of the inquiry are just as important.

The questions that teachers and administrators ask are as varied as the issues that impinge upon them. This is not surprising given that teaching involves a combination of scientific knowledge, craftsmanship, and artistry and that learning appears to be at times predictable and on other occasions elusive and mysterious. The following is a sampling of questions related to curriculum, instruction, assessment, learning, and programs pursued by teachers and administrators I have worked with recently. Within each category, I have included questions that vary in their depth and scope.

Questions about curriculum:

- How rigorous is our science curriculum?
- What percentage of the foreign language curriculum should be devoted to the language lab?

- What are the strengths and weaknesses of my language arts curriculum?
- Are we implementing all the components of the new mathematics curriculum effectively?

Questions about instruction:

- How can I incorporate thinking skills into my lessons?
- How can we adapt lessons for middle school students with special needs?
- How do we determine the effectiveness of different instructional approaches?
- How well are we using differentiated instruction in high school science classes?

Questions about assessment:

- How can I help teachers in my school reconcile classroom with state assessment data?
- How do I tailor my assessments to address different learning styles in my class?
- How will the job-embedded performance evaluation process work with new teachers in the district?
- How can we improve the kinds of assessments that we use in the primary grades?

Questions about learning:

- In what contexts are students using their minds well?
- How will peer response groups affect the quality of writing that my students produce?
- What kinds of critical thinking skills are students capable of, and which skills do they struggle with?
- What will we learn about students' understanding of the content covered in class through reading their portfolios?

Questions about programs:

- To what extent do the teachers in my building believe that our professional development offerings are driven by their needs?
- How consistent is my math program with state standards?
- In what ways does our technology program support the use of instructional technology in different subjects?
- How well are we using our two different literacy programs in the upper elementary grades?

THREE EXAMPLES OF INQUIRY

To illustrate the nuances and possibilities of individual, collaborative, and school-based inquiry, I have selected three case studies that involve one of the most significant problems for many educators and schools: the problem of using test data effectively. This problem reveals the tension that exists because standardized tests and teachers' engaging curriculum and instruction are not always a good match. Rich activities and interactions are too often surrendered when students are obliged to take a standardized test.

All three case studies were prompted by the belief that it is possible to increase students' performance on tests without teaching to the test items themselves, even though many teachers and administrators believe that the best strategy for increasing scores involves having students learn the test items in isolation and experience the test demands prior to taking the test.

Despite their different approaches, all three studies sought to develop a process whereby teachers would have much greater control over the strategies they used to prepare students for standardized state tests, while at the same time gaining new knowledge about the effectiveness of those strategies on students' learning. These are all serious studies done by classroom teachers in "ordinary" circumstances. Each study indicates what small groups of teachers or an individual can do. Clearly, there are limits on a teacher's time, so this work is often done as part of a staff development effort.

An Example of Individual Inquiry

Shirley Glickman is a school-based staff developer who works in Community School District 10 in the Bronx, New York. For the past 2 years, she has encouraged teachers to develop and use scoring rubrics with students to diagnose and monitor students' writing progress and achievement (Glickman, 2002). She believes that students' use of these rubrics will ultimately help them assess their strengths and weaknesses as writers and improve their writing. At the same time, she is concerned that students perform well on the state's English language arts (ELA) test and focuses much of her time as a professional developer helping teachers prepare students for such tests. Her action research questions were: "To what extent will students' use of classroom-based criteria charts, writing rubrics, and reflection affect their understanding of what is good work?" and "How does the use of criteria charts, rubrics, and reflection affect students' performance and revision of work?"

Shirley developed a protocol of 10 lessons aimed at helping students use criteria charts, rubrics, and reflections on writing work. It began with a lesson where students examined selected texts and used them to brainstorm criteria charts for content, organization, style, and mechanics. In the second and third lessons, students used the language from the criteria charts to draft a four-level rubric for content, organization, style, and mechanics that appears in Table 3.1.

Lesson 4 involved having students score anonymous work using the rubrics they had developed, and Lesson 5 used the same process, only this time students assessed their practice test for the statewide ELA assessment. In Lesson 6, students developed a plan for revising the work they scored in the form of a letter to themselves. In Lesson 7, they carried out their revisions, and in Lesson 8, they assessed that work using the rubric. In Lesson 9, students wrote a reflection on their work and on their perception of their future performance on the statewide test. This reflection included the following four prompts:

1. I think I will get a _____ on the ELA test.

2. In order to get this I need to . . .

3. The part that will be easy for me will be . . .

4. The part that will be hard for me will be . . .

In Lesson 10 students conferenced with their teacher. The focus of this conference was an item from their reflection centered on the student's perceptions of the part of the state test that would be difficult.

Table 3.1   Rubric for the Writing Response for Fourth-Grade English Language Arts, P.S. 24

	4	*3*	*2*	*1*
Content	I answered <u>all</u> parts of the question.	I answered <u>most</u> parts of the question. I could write a bit more.	I answered a <u>few</u> parts of the question. I need to reread and write more.	I didn't answer the question. I need to reread to understand the question better.
	I used <u>a lot</u> of details and examples to support my opinion.	I used <u>some</u> details and examples to support my opinion. I could add a bit more.	I used a <u>few</u> details and examples to support my opinion. I need to find more details and examples.	I didn't use details and examples to support my opinion. I need to reread and underline details to use.
	I am <u>totally</u> focused. All my sentences help answer the question.	I am <u>mostly</u> focused on the topic. I need to reread to see what I could add or take out.	I am <u>not so</u> focused on the topic. I need to reread my topic sentence when I'm writing.	I'm not sure what my topic is. I need to decide what my topic is.
Organization	My paragraphs have a topic sentence, detail sentences, and a closing sentence.	My paragraphs have an opening sentence and detail sentences. I need a closing sentence.	I have detail sentences. I need opening and closing sentences.	I need help understanding how to write a paragraph.
	<u>All</u> my information is in logical order.	<u>Most</u> of my information is in logical order.	I need to put my ideas in better order.	I need help putting my ideas in good order.
	I tied <u>all</u> my ideas together with transition/time/sequence words.	I used <u>some</u> transition/time/sequence words.	I only used one or two transition/time/sequence words.	I need help with transition/time/sequence words.
Style	I used $100 words.	I used $50 words.	I used favorite words.	I used simple words.
	I used <u>many</u> different kinds of sentences.	I used <u>some</u> different kinds of sentences.	My sentences are mostly the same.	I need help writing different kinds of sentences.
	I sound like I'm excited about the topic.	I sound like I'm interested in the topic.	It's hard to tell if I'm interested in the topic.	I sound like I don't care about the topic at all.
Mechanics	I used capitals and punctuation correctly.	I <u>mostly</u> used capitals and punctuation correctly.	I used <u>some</u> capitals and punctuation correctly.	I didn't use capitals and punctuation correctly.
	Most words are spelled correctly. <u>All</u> easy words are spelled correctly.	<u>Most</u> words are spelled correctly.	I used <u>some</u> good spelling.	I hardly used good spelling.
	I indented <u>all</u> paragraphs.	I indented <u>most</u> paragraphs.	I indented <u>some</u> paragraphs.	I didn't indent.

Shirley implemented her protocol between October and December 2001 in four fourth-grade classes in her school with the support of the classroom teachers who taught the children every day. Throughout the year, she collected a comprehensive array of data from these classes. These data included

- Pre-intervention rubric scores for content and mechanics on a practice language arts test
- Post-intervention rubric scores for students' revised written responses
- Students' predictions of their language arts state test scores prior to taking the test
- Students' reflections on what they needed to do to succeed, what they thought would be difficult, and what they thought would be easy
- Actual language arts state test scores
- Students' perceptions on the value of the lesson protocol they experienced
- Teachers' perceptions on the value of the protocol and the staff development that supported its use
- Teachers' perceptions on the effect of the protocol on students' performance in writing and attitudes towards writing and revision

I am including some of Shirley's results based on the analysis of one of the fourth-grade classes she worked with extensively.

Students' performance on the pre-protocol practice test in October was significantly different from their performance on the post-protocol revision in December. In October, their mean score for content was 1.53, and their mean score for mechanics was 2.66. In December, their mean score for content was 3.44, and their mean score for mechanics was 3.44.

Students' performance on the pre-protocol practice test was also significantly different from their performance on the actual language arts state test. Their mean scores for content increased from a 1.53 to 2.83. Their mean scores for mechanics increased from 2.66 to 3.44.

Students' scores on the post-protocol revision were nearly identical to their scores on the actual state test. Their predicted scores on their state tests (a mean of 3.57) were not far from their actual scores (3.14).

In addition to providing compelling data on the effects of implemented protocol on students' performance, the study yielded rich and substantive insights about students' thinking. The analysis of students' reflections on what they needed to do to attain their predicted performance on the state test revealed a comprehensive understanding of the rubric indicators.

When reflecting on the parts of the test that would be easy, students most often identified issues related to mechanics, frequently mentioning spelling, punctuation, capitalization, and paragraphing. Many students also stated that it would be easy to include details and examples from the text.

Students' reflections on the parts of the test that would be difficult centered on content and style. The most common responses to this prompt included staying focused on the topic, using sophisticated vocabulary, and making the writing interesting for the reader.

When assessing the value of the protocol to support their learning about writing, students had much to say as well. Many of them stated that the rubric and its use in self-assessment provided them with clear expectations for their written work. One typical response was "It showed me what they expeked of me."

Students also valued the rubric's specificity in the dimension descriptors because it gave them the language they could use to improve their own performance, as is evident in the following responses:

"The rubric helped me to improve my writing by telling me all the steps in getting a 4."

"The rubric helped me grow my writing."

Students also stated that the rubric and its use gave them the tools they needed to effectively assess themselves, "to know how good the writing was."

Students were able to use the examples of leveled responses and sample texts to generate explicit performance criteria and as additional tools for self-assessment.

"I got to see what an outstanding essay looked like and what a horrible essay looked like."

"I have a good way to show myself if I'm right or wrong."

They also credited the rubric and analysis for giving them confidence in their ability to perform successfully on the state test:

"Now I will feel confertable and I won't think it will be so hard like I did in the beginning."

Students also valued the revision process and saw it as an opportunity to apply their new learning:

"Thank you for letting me write a revision. I think every student should have a rubric in there class."

Students' reflections confirmed the usefulness of the protocol in providing them with clear expectations for students' writing and with specific self-assessment and revision tools. The data indicate that students enjoyed working through the process of writing and revising their work, this being a significant feat for any teacher working with elementary school students.

Teachers were also invited to evaluate the protocol with questions such as:

- How comfortable are you with the protocol? Please explain.
- How will you implement the protocol in your classroom next year?
- What additional support do you need to implement it?
- Describe changes in your students' writing that you attribute to the implementation of the protocol.
- Describe changes in students' attitudes toward writing the written parts of the language arts state test that you attribute to the implementation of the protocol.

The analysis of the data from the preceding questions revealed an overwhelmingly positive response. Teachers embraced the protocol and committed to using it and, in many cases, expanding it to incorporate the creation of rubrics in areas other than writing.

Teachers also attributed many changes in their students' writing to the protocol. Following are some illustrations.

- "Clearer focus, better understanding of what writing is, they learned how to write for a reader."
- "The were able to monitor their own writing. For example, if they received a '2,' they knew why and were able to make corrections."
- "At times they were more responsible for their own work. The 'revision period' is where students extend themselves."

Teachers also saw important changes in students' attitudes:

- "Students were willing to take charge, they can tell what is acceptable and unacceptable and <u>why</u>."
- "I believe they have an increased sense of confidence, having discovered the 'secret' to good writing. They were able to predict their score and know what was needed to improve it."

Nothing speaks louder for the success of this study than the students' work. I had a difficult time selecting the work I wanted to include here because Shirley had one compelling example of students' work after another. I selected the work of a child we will name David, a fourth grader. His performance usually falls in the top quadrant of his class, although he suffers from Asperger's syndrome. David's strength in writing has always been in mechanics, whereas his content is rather weak. Following is his practice test taken in October 2001.

The fable teaches that if you want something, you have to work hard for it because the dog asked the wolf to work for the master to get food to eat. **(Rubric scores: content, 2; mechanics, 4)**

The following is David's response to an exercise in which students were to list ideas for improving their own writing in the form of a letter to themselves, using the rubric found in Table 3.2:

Dear self,

Write more. Include D.S. [detail sentences] and C.S. [closing sentences]. Put more sentences in. Put more details and examples. <u>ANSWER THE QUESTION!!</u>

Put information in logical order. Add $100 words. Add more sentences. Excite writer.

The following is David's revised writing sample, produced on December 2001:

The fable teaches that if you want something, you have to work hard for it. The dog asked the wolf to work for the master. Then he could get food to eat.

The wolf thought that work would be a cinch. The dog was very well-fed. Actually, the work was more tiring than other he <u>did</u> by himself.

The dog got so much food because he had been guarding the master's house. Then, the wolf ran back into the forest. But even though the wolf didn't get any food at the master's house, the wolf can still find food in the forest.

Maybe a bird. At least I think a bird is easy to hunt. Well, for a fleet-footed animal.

Table 3.2   Students' Self-Evaluation Sheet for Writing Sample, Based on Level 4 of the Fourth-Grade English Language Arts Rubric

Rubric Category	Rubric Description	Evidence/Proof From Student Sample
Content	All parts of the question are answered.	No
	The answer has a lot of details and examples.	No
	The answer is totally focused. All answers help answer the question.	No
Organization	Answer has a topic sentence, detail sentences, and a closing sentence.	T.S. (topic sentence) No D.S. (detail sentences) or C.S. (closing sentences)
	All information is in logical order.	No
	Ideas are tied together with transition/time/sequence words.	No
	There are some $100 words.	No
	There are different kinds of sentences (long, short, different beginnings).	One long sentence
	Sounds like the writer is excited about the topic.	No way, Jose!
Mechanics	Capital letters and punctuation are used correctly.	Yeah, Baby!
	Most words are spelled correctly. All easy words are spelled correctly.	Yeah, Baby!
	All paragraphs are indented.	Yeah, Baby!

You need to work hard whenever you want something. That's what this fable teaches.
   (Rubric scores: content, 4; mechanics, 4)

David's reflections predicting his test scores are shown below:

1. I think I will get a **3.50** on the ELA.

2. In order to get this I need to: **focus well and put lots of details and examples.**

3. The part that will be easy for me will be: **indenting.**

4. The part that will be hard for me will be: **probably adding and taking out.**

David accurately assessed his performance on the state test. His score was actually 3.5. He was also accurate in assessing the change from his pretest in October to his revised work in December, as is evident in the answer to the question "How did using the rubric and the analysis help you to improve your writing?"

Maybe it was the details and examples. My first Dog and Wolf piece was brief. My second was just about chock full of details and examples.

An Example of Collaborative Inquiry

One of the goals of CSETL is to help teachers document and use best practice. Unfortunately, the increased attention to state and other standardized tests has made it difficult for teachers and administrators, especially in low-performing schools, to focus on best practice. Instead, students are constantly bombarded with test preparation activities that are often devoid of meaningful content. The question that five fellows and I pursued was: "What does it look like to teach students strategies to address test demands without teaching to the test itself?" The teachers spanned Grades 1 through 4 and 8. Two of them were reading/ language arts specialists who worked with teachers in their classrooms as well as pulling out students for remediation. Three others were teachers in self-contained classrooms.

We designed the study in July 2000 during a 5-day summer institute and implemented it in the fall of the same year. Teachers then met for 4 days over the course of the year to do the scoring and analysis of the data and to discuss the results. Having had direct experience with New York State's new language arts test that was introduced in 1999, we recognized that one of the test demands that students struggled with the most was elaboration: the ability to support statements with relevant details.

We designed a two-part pre-test and two-part post-test to measure changes in students' use of relevant details in a 3-week span. The tests were parallel in structure. The first part of the pretest was to "describe a leaf"; the second part of the pretest, administered on the next day, asked students to "describe the same leaf for a person who cannot see it." Students were told that they were to try to do their best in this writing and that teachers would analyze their work to develop strategies to help them become better writers.

The first part of the post-test asked students to "describe a cookie"; the second part, administered on the next day, asked them to "describe the same cookie for someone who cannot taste it." We expected the second part of the pretest and posttest to elicit greater elaboration than the first part of the pretest and post-test.

We brainstormed different strategies for teaching students to elaborate on their ideas in writing, including using such graphic organizers as webs and charts, drawing and creating images, using the five senses to produce information on an object or subject, and specific timed prewriting activities. Following is a brief description of each strategy and its implementation.

• Following the administration of the pretests, one language arts teacher asked fourth-grade students if they had done any prewriting activities. When students said that they hadn't, the teacher reviewed three prewriting strategies: brainstorming, drawing, and webbing. Over a period of 3 days, the teacher structured his or her writing lessons with an initial whole-class discussion and teacher modeling of one of these prewriting strategies, followed by a period of individual student practice using one of the three strategies for 2 minutes. The lesson ended with teacher-guided prompts to help students reflect on the value of that strategy for them.

• Following an initial review of web graphic organizers, eighth-grade students generated a web to guide their writing of a paragraph describing a hard candy. The teacher collected these paragraphs and identified a set of good and not-so-good initial sentences to guide the elaboration of ideas within a paragraph. Students reviewed the lists, selected the three best initial sentences, and discussed the merits of their selection. The teacher emphasized the idea that initial sentences often determine the content of the paragraph.

• In a third-grade class, the teacher reviewed the five senses with her students by describing her relationship with a blind friend and how that relationship requires the teacher to paint pictures with words for her friend. The teacher then read observational poetry by Valerie Wirth to her students. Students then described objects on the science table orally and in writing. A follow-up activity involved using words to create images of specific students and having the class use those images to identify the person each image represented. A similar activity involved tasting fruits and using words to describe the experience.

• In a first- and second-grade class, a reading specialist used a think-aloud approach and a graphic organizer to help students describe an autumn scarecrow doll. Holding up a picture book, she asked about the picture on the cover: "Who are the characters in this picture?" Then, as she went through the book, she asked, "What are the characters doing? What is the setting of this picture? Where and when does it take place? What do you think the characters are thinking or feeling? Explain your answer. What do you think will happen next?"

Each teacher selected one of these strategies and agreed to teach it for 3 weeks in between the two-part pretest and the two-part posttest. After administering the two-part pretest in September, each of the five teachers identified seven students who spanned the range of ability, gender, and motivation in each of his or her classes (one teacher had two classes, so six classes were drawn from). The 42 students selected constitute the sample for this study.

To score students' responses, we first counted the number of relevant words in the first part of the pretest and posttest. In the second part of the pretest and posttest, we counted only the number of additional relevant words. A relevant word was a noun, verb, or adjective that related to the prompt (e.g., *oven* or *crunchy*). Words and phrases that were unrelated to the prompt (e.g., "This is the end" or "Then I look for an anthill with a friend") were not counted. Two of us scored three students together and discussed our scores aloud as we worked through the papers. Then we each scored independently. We rescored all the students' work where there was a discrepancy, and we asked each of the other members of the group to review the scores as well.

To analyze the data, we looked at the increases or decreases in the number of relevant descriptive words generated in the two-part pretest and posttest. Table 3.3 shows that older students generated more words than younger students and that some students did not generate more relevant words in the second part of the pretest measure or in the second part of the posttest measure, whereas others did. There was no consistency in the shifts from the first to the second parts of the pretest and posttest. In a few cases, students generated more words in the second part of the pretest or posttest, but in many others they generated fewer words.

The following examples illustrate the lack of consistency in the patterns of growth on the different tests (students' writing is given verbatim). Below are two examples from students whose number of relevant words increased from the first to the second part of the pretest:

1. Second Grader

First Part of Pretest: "A leave has lines on saertint parts of the leaves"

Second Part of Pretest: "A leave is green and they are difrint shaps and sisis. In the fal the leavs chang colors and they fall."

2. Eighth Grader

First Part of Pretest:
"All different flavors
Gently falls at autumn
The ride of life
Gusts of wispy wind
Twigs surround its path
Winter melts away
Then once again, blooms it's next ride."

Second Part of Pretest: "A leaf is a plant that blossoms gradually during the 4 seasons. When picking a leaf from a stem, it is so fragile and gentle that with a slight tug it can tear instantly. It can slice right down the middle through its veins crispy and sharp. When running your fingers against it you can feel the smallest vines rub against your skin. Depending on the weather, and the changing of seasons, leaves can go from an orange red to a bright green. Sometimes, just in one tree there could be an assortment of colors. Green, yellow, brown, red, or orange, even purple. When winter rolls around, the leaves shrivel and dry out, so when stepping on them they can crackle like crackers."

The following is an example from a student, an eighth grader, whose number of relevant words decreased from the first to the second part of the pretest:

First Part of Pretest: "A leaf has roots in it. Its green in the summer yellow and red in the fall and brown in the winter. leaves fall from high trees from the cold winds of fall and winter to the horrible storms of summer. When in the winter as you steep on one of them, make a crunchy noise like when you chew potato chips."

Second Part of Pretest: "The leaves are red in winter and fall they have brown spots and are very crunchy."

The following is an example from a student, a fourth grader, whose number of relevant words increased between the pretest and the posttest:

Second Part of Pretest: "The leaf is green its a big leaf. It's a wet leaf and it's on the ground. It's a weird leaf because it is straight."

Second Part of Posttest: "The cookie tastes like cookie dough. It has raisings it has oatmeal sugar on it. The oatmeal sugar tastes like sugar but with a little bit of spice. The chocolate chips tastes like chocolate. Choclate tastes good because it melts in your mouth. Raisons taste good because they come from grapes."

We then looked at the changes from pretests to posttests, as well as the kinds of students who made the most positive gains. Table 2.4 shows that different kinds of students benefited from different strategies. In some classes, the students who made the most gains had the lowest abilities, whereas in others, gains were made across the ability spectrum. In Grades 1 through 3 and in one of the fourth-grade classes, the students who benefited the most from the writing strategies were of low to middle ability. In the other fourth-grade class and in the eighth-grade classes, above-average students changed the most.

Table 3.3   Number of Words Generated in the Pretests and Posttests

Teacher and Grade	Pretest	Posttest	Total No. of Additional Words Generated Between Pretests and Posttests	% Gained Between Pretests and Posttests	No. of Students Who Generated More Words in the First Part of the Posttest Than the First Part of the Pretest	No. of Students Who Generated More Words in the Second Part of the Posttest Than the Second Part of the Pretest	Comments
Carol (Reading), Grade 1	Part 1: 9 Part 2: 15	Part 1: 23 Part 2: 16	14 1	60.8 6.29	5	2	Most overall change by middle-ability students
Carol (Reading), Grade 2	Part 1: 29 Part 2: 33	Part 1: 90 Part 2: 31	61 -2	67.7 -6.06	5	3	Most change by one low- and two middle-ability students
Alex, Grade 3	Part 1: 69 Part 2: 58	Part 1: 93 Part 2: 53	24 -5	25.8 -8.6	4	3	Changes in low-, middle-, and high-ability students
Karen, Grade 4	Part 1: 127 Part 2: 36	Part 1: 90 Part 2: 54	-37 18	-29.13 33.3	3	4	Most change by lowest-ability students
Vicki (Language Arts), Grade 4	Part 1: 135 Part 2: 81	Part 1: 92 Part 2: 56	-43 -29	-31.8 -30.8	2	1	Most change by above-average- and average-ability students
Linda, Grade 8	Part 1: 189 Part 2: 154	Part 1: 260 Part 2: 141	71 -13	27.3 -8.44	6	4	Most changes by above-average and resource room students

Our initial analysis of the data confused us somewhat, but it also prompted us to ask deeper questions about the study and about students. Our second analysis was qualitative. It involved reexamining the qualities of the students' responses to the pretest and posttest and exploring the nature of the word choices made by students in these tests. These data are summarized in Table 3.4.

The data in Table 3.4 support the notion that elaboration is not only about writing more details. It is also about focus and audience awareness. For example, following are two examples of students whose number of words did not change significantly from pretest to posttest but whose writing improved markedly. The first example is from a fourth grader whose pretest and posttest writings are comparable in length. However, his writing in the second posttest indicates that his choice of words is influenced by knowing that the person for whom he is describing a cookie cannot taste it.

> **Second Part of Pretest**: "A leaf is a thing hanging out of a tree. It is green and can be other colors in different seasons. It is easy to rip the tree brings nutrition to the leaf so the leaf can stay healthy. The leaf is not some thing to eat. It feels smooth. The leafs fall down at winter. In fall leafs looks like fire."

> **Second Part of Posttest**: "A cookie tastes like a little flat circle food made out of dough. It tastes like a crunchy and hard biscuit. It can be brown and yellow. It is very sticky. My favorite kind is chocolate chip. I like eating cookies. You can smell it so you could imagine how it tastes."

The second example is from an eighth grader whose number of words decreased from the first part of the pretest to the first part of the posttest but whose writing clearly improved in terms of its focus on the sense of taste in the second part of the posttest.

> **Second Part of Pretest**: "A leaf is a plant that blossoms gradually during the 4 seasons. When picking a leaf from a stem, it is so fragile and gentle that with a slight tug it can tear instantly. It can slice right down the middle through its veins crisply and sharp. When running your fingers against it you can feel the smallest vines rub against your skin. Depending on the weather, and the changing of seasons leaves can go from a orange red to a bright green. Sometimes just in one tree these could be an asortment of colors, green, yellow, brown, red or orange, even purple. When winter rolls around the leaves shrink and dry out, so when stepping on them they can crackle like crackers."

> **Second Part of Posttest**: "The choclate chip cookie tastes very much the way it smells. The dough tastes a bitter but sweet cookie. The crumbs left on your tongue always leave you a delicious after taste. The choclate chips give your mouth a sugar rush. The choclate tastes like melted smooth fudge. Strong and scrumptous. The last bite always makes you hungry for more, leaving your stomach with a warm, appetizing and full feeling."

As we examined the writing from all students, we noticed that they varied in their interpretation of the second part of the pretest and posttest prompt. Some students assumed that the reader needed sensory data about sight in the second part of the pretest and about taste

Table 3.4   Qualitative Assessment of Students' Responses

Changes From First Part of Pretest to Second Part of Pretest

Grade	Language Content	Language Structure
Grade 1 Picture prompt, graphic organizer	Five out of seven added details in the second part of the pretest	Same for both tests
Grade 2 Picture prompt, graphic organizer	Four used different details in the second part of the pretest; two added details; one stayed the same	Same for both tests
Grade 3 Observation and modeling	Two performed better on the second part of the pretest; five treated the second part of the pretest as an extension of the first part instead of writing a new answer	Same for both tests, or more focused on task during second part of pretest
Grade 4 (Karen) Visualization	Four used different details; two wrote less in the second part of pretest; one stayed the same	One wrote sentences in the first part of the pretest and a paragraph in the second part of the pretest. One did not use any sentences
Grade 4 (Vicki) Timed prewrite	Five used different senses in the second part of pretest; one was more focused on the second part of the pretest; one performed the same on both parts	Same for both tests
Grade 8 Exemplary topic sentences	Five out of seven focused more on second part of pretest; one performed the same on both parts; one changed genre	More effective use of similes, metaphors, etc., in first part of pretest

Changes from Second Part of Pretest to Second Part of Posttest

Grade	Language Content	Language Structure
Grade 1	Three gave more precise details in second part of posttest; one gave different details; one gave fewer details; two performed the same on both tests	Three wrote more precise sentences in second part of posttest
Grade 2	Six were more focused in second part of posttest; three gave more details in second part of posttest; two gave fewer details in second part of posttest	
Grade 3	Three gave more details in second part of posttest; one was more focused on second part of posttest; two reworded for second part of posttest; one used more precision in second part of posttest	
Grade 4 (Karen)	Four gave more focused description in second part of posttest; one simply repeated; one was more general in second part of posttest; one gave less description in second part of posttest	Three had more sentence structure in second part of posttest
Grade 4 (Vicki)	Three were more focused in second part of posttest; one gave more description in second part of posttest; two performed the same on both tests	Language structure was the same on both tests
Grade 8	Two were more artistic in second part of pretest; one wrote less but with greater focus on taste in second part of posttest	All performed the same on both tests

in the second part of the posttest. Others assumed that because the readers could neither "see" nor "taste," they needed sensory information about other senses. The different interpretations reminded us that knowledge and meaning are individually and socially constructed and that fairly simple prompts can elicit different interpretations.

We rediscovered that vocabulary increased with age but also that older students made more personal cognitive and affective connections with the written tasks. Their writing had greater depth, showed greater variety in language structure and use, and included more imagery and figurative language than the writing of younger students, particularly students in Grades 1 through 3. The comparison of students of different ages showed us how much some aspects of writing are affected by age and diverse experiences.

In exploring the different motivations students had toward completing the pretests and posttests, we learned that first and second graders were comfortable, and even eager, to complete the second part of the pretest and posttest. On the other hand, many of the students in Grades 3, 4, and 8 found the second part of the pretest and posttest redundant, believing that their lessons and activities were events rather than processes to be revisited. This explained some of the differences and apparent decreases in the students' writing from the first to the second part of the pretests and posttests. It also reminded us of the inherent problems associated with traditional test preparation practices and with on-demand tests, both of which often preclude contextualized or purposeful writing.

As we discussed and compared each of the strategies used, we discovered that all the strategies produced positive changes in one or more of the students but that none worked for everyone. This conclusion is tentative, for a longer period between the pretest and posttest may be needed to produce greater and more positive changes for more students.

Our study was limited by the different interpretations of the prompt by students and by the fact that our sample of teachers was far from even, including classroom teachers and language arts specialists. Nonetheless, it provided us with a rich forum for the exploration of students' writing, of elaboration as a complex skill, of the relationship between stimulus (prompts) and responses, and of the importance of looking at student data from multiple angles. We rediscovered some of the inherent complexities of teaching writing and the significant value of teachers' sharing and discussing students' work.

Our study led us to an increased repertoire of teaching strategies and convinced us that all teachers can benefit from collaborative studies in which they control for some variation in their teaching and assessment practices aimed at producing specific learning outcomes.

An Example of School-Based Inquiry

Jeanette Atkinson, a CSETL fellow and staff developer at the Genesee Valley Board of Cooperative Educational Services in New York, and I have implemented a school-based action research study in a PreK–8 building in Buffalo, New York. The Buffalo study was informed by an action research study initiated in Dansville, a small rural school serving Grades 3 through 5 in upstate New York. Both schools have been guided by the same general research question: "How can the use of state test data and the analysis of students' performance on state tests help teachers diagnose specific learning needs and tests demand and then help design and monitor strategies to address them?"

The study has been implemented through four stages in both schools. The remaining descriptions are based solely on the implementation of these stages in the Buffalo school. In Buffalo, the action research study began in September 2001 with all the teachers in Grades

Table 3.5   Summary of Fourth-Grade Test Demands

Part 1 *From Sampler*	Session 2 *From 2001 Test*	Session 3 *From 2001 Test*
Planning	**Planning**	**Planning**

Identify main idea
Use context clues
Read questions prior to
  reading story
Manage footnotes
Understand and read graphic
  organizers
	Use notes
	Practice note writing
	Organize ideas
	Use graphic organizers
		Identify sentences or phrases in
		  both passages that support
		  student's opinion
		Discriminate relevant from
		  irrelevant information
		Reread directions and questions

Development of Ideas	**Development of Ideas**	**Development of Ideas**

Synthesize information
Establish cause-and-effect
  relationships
Use context clues
	Notice beginning/middle/end
	Use notes
		Use first reading to support opinion
		Connect the task directions with a
		  reading that may not support
		  them (read between the lines)
		Incorporate information from two
		  genres
		Write and develop an opinion

Organization	**Organization**	**Organization**

Present ideas in logical order
Read graphic organizers
	Recognize the sequence of events
	  (many stages of story)
		Recognize the sequence of events
		  (many stages of story)

Language Use/Comprehension	**Language Use/Comprehension**	**Language Use/Comprehension**

	Manage unfamiliar vocabulary in the
	  passages
	Reading may be too difficult for some
		Decode unfamiliar vocabulary
		  in texts

Mechanics/Conventions	**Mechanics/Conventions**	**Mechanics/Conventions**

	Notice:
	  – Spelling
	  – End marks
	  – Capitalization	

Test-Taking Strategies	**Test-Taking Strategies**	**Test-Taking Strategies**
		Read directions Look at the parts of the answers that have been scaffolded for help
Other	**Other**	**Other**

Identify author's point of view	Note: Length of passage requires
	  multiple steps to remember for
	  future use in test
	Practice using memory	

3 through 8. In the first stage, teachers took the fourth- and eighth-grade New York State language arts tests that were administered the year before. Teachers in Grades 3 and 4 took the fourth-grade test, and teachers in Grades 5 through 8 took the eighth-grade test and noted the test's specific demands: planning, idea development or elaboration, organization, use of language, use of conventions, and test-taking strategies. They also identified any confusing or misleading items. A summary of the test demands that they identified for the fourth grade is included in Table 3.5.

Next, teachers worked in groups of four. Each group included teachers from two adjacent grade levels, a special education teacher, and a reading teacher. Over a 90-minute period, they analyzed completed student test booklets from four pairs of students, each pair of whom had received a different score in the state test the year before (within a given pair, both students had the same score). In New York, students can receive an overall score that goes from 1 to 4. The purposes of such analysis were to determine (a) what students at each level knew and could do; (b) what their specific struggles were; and (c) what all students could do regardless of the scores they received. A partial summary of these data is presented in Table 3.6.

Having analyzed the test as well as students' test booklets enabled teachers to identify and discuss the needs of different kinds of students. This provided a context that allowed them to understand the printouts of state test results from the prior 2 years and to compare such results with the information they had gleaned through their own analysis. Teachers concluded that all students needed much help with basic reading and writing instruction and that students at all levels scored very low on elaboration or development of ideas. They also found that students lacked specific strategies to unpack texts.

In Stage 2 of this work, each teacher selected seven or eight students who represented the diversity within his or her classroom: three of low ability, two of moderate ability, and two of high ability. In addition, the sample included other sources of variability, including gender, race, motivation, and family history or issues. Teachers created a folder for each of these students and identified his or her specific needs. Our plan was to use these folders in all subsequent meetings to monitor teachers' use of strategies to support specific learning needs.

The second part of Stage 2 included the identification of instructional strategies that would target specific learning needs. Because some of the teachers in this school lacked a strong background in language arts teaching, I secured additional support from a district literacy consultant so that teachers would learn new strategies and not just brainstorm what they already knew. We expected teachers to be able to connect specific strategies to different student needs and to record the strategy(ies) to be targeted on each of the student folders.

In Stage 3, teachers conducted an analysis of state standards and required curriculum guidelines and reconciled their identified student needs against them. They identified teaching and assessment gaps in all four language arts standards and performance indicators. We kept a list of each individual teacher's gaps so that we could eventually measure their progress in addressing standards.

Shortly after this gap analysis process, we asked teachers to generate and discuss lessons and activities aimed at addressing performance indicators they had previously ignored while at the same time helping students incorporate different reading and writing strategies into their learning repertoire. This stage included discussions, among teachers who shared the same grade level, that revolved around the analysis and comparison of different teaching strategies and their effectiveness with different types of students. It also included cross-grade conversations regarding the extent to which specific strategies were more or less appropriate for different grade levels.

The conversations that teachers held with each other revealed some of the flawed assumptions in our work. Teachers were not as experienced as we thought in working collaboratively to analyze and discuss data, and it was difficult for them to engage in sustained conversations about students' work. For example, due to misconceptions in understanding literacy, many of the teachers were unable to recognize and label precise students' needs and

Table 3.6   Partial Summary of Student Data From Analysis of Work From Four Scored Levels

Level 1 Students	Level 2 Students

Planning
  – No planning
  – Some random notes, but it is hard to see the connection to reading
  – Use of one or more complete sentences with partial webs
  – No underlining of passage
	Planning
	  – Incomplete or poor use of graphic organizer (including both relevant and irrelevant information)
	  – Some prewriting
	  – Underlining of relevant words in passage

Development of ideas
  – Poor and confusing development
  – Some evidence of imagination
  – Little if any detail
	Development of ideas
	  – Lack of details
	  – Completion of organizers
	  – No comparison of articles

Organization
  – Random or disorganized note taking
  – Confusing
	Organization
	  – Beginning organization
	  – Confusing; list of facts; lack of detail

Comprehension skills/strategies
  – Poor sequencing
	Comprehension skills/strategies
	  – Understanding can be inferred
	  – Basic knowledge of passage
	  – Difficulties putting information together

Language use
  – Poor language use
	Language use
	  – Writes a sentence; some incomplete sentences
	  – No paragraph structure
	  – Poor grammar, spelling, vocabulary
	  – Weak sentence structure

Test strategies
  – Can read something
  – Prewriting can be inferred
	Test strategies
	  – Finishes test
	  – Can read story
	  – Some prewriting

therefore had no context from which to build instructional strategies to target them. This finding led us to a shift in our activities from an exclusive focus on the analysis of students' folders to the incorporation of demonstrations of literacy strategies and lessons for the remainder of the school year.

Such sessions included information on assessment design, with an emphasis on the development of diagnostic and formative assessment measures, standards-based lesson design, strategy-focused lesson development and implementation, and the incorporation of choice into lessons and assessments. We also modeled lessons in all the different grade levels and in the self-contained special education classes. Though the shift in our focus increased their uses of literacy strategies, it also resulted in less attention to our collaborative inquiry.

In the culmination of Stage 3, teachers were asked to use insights from a year-long exploration and analysis of student work to reevaluate their commitment to the continued exploration of literacy strategies aimed at addressing students' needs. They all reaffirmed this commitment, and in the summer I analyzed all the student folders from 12 teachers in Grades 3 through 8 to ground my understanding of the work we needed to do.

Among the positive findings from this review were that in all classes graphic organizers were used as prewriting strategies. In at least five classes, teachers used many of the literacy strategies we modeled. They also incorporated student self-assessment. Four entries in the folders showed that teachers asked students to personalize the material learned or to find a real-world connection. Finally, their mathematics entries were varied and included evidence of attention to problem-solving strategies.

On the negative side, all but four of the assessments included in the folders lacked authenticity and were derived from textbooks and other educational materials. They also lacked opportunities for students to personalize material or use their preferred learning style. The overall emphasis of teachers' lessons was organization, conventions, and comprehension, whereas voice, idea development, and focus were ignored. For the most part, teachers lacked explicit performance criteria for the work they included and were inconsistent in the criteria they used for different students in their classrooms. I only found one example of assessment data being used to determine or modify instruction. Perhaps the most striking finding was that it was sometimes difficult to differentiate the work of elementary school children from the work of middle schoolers.

One of the similarities among the three inquiries that I have described in this chapter is that they all left the authors with more questions than they answered. As is often the case with systematic inquiry, especially in the human arena, we quickly discover the complexity of what we are exploring and realize how little we truly know. Each of the questions we ask generates a partial answer and at least two more questions, triggering what appears to be an endless quest for a truth that will always escape us.

Shirley Glickman's reflection upon completing the first phase of her research sums up this process better than I could:

> As my initial curiosity grew into an abiding interest, and then blossomed into a full blown passion, I found myself wanting more and more information about what students were thinking, about what teachers were thinking, about the learning itself. Each time I designed a reflection, I realized I needed another. Each time I added a new column of data to my spreadsheet, I realized I needed to add another column. I ran out of space and moved onto another sheet, and still the questions bombarded me: *Where did the learning go forward? Where did the learning stop (high tide)? Where did it seemingly recede?* And of course, the underlying and overriding question: *Why?*
>
> At one point, I asked myself: When will the journey end, and what will my destination, my "final product," look like?
>
> And my response was: You will <u>never</u> be done, you will <u>always</u> have more questions: and furthermore, perhaps it is not the final product that has exclusive value. Perhaps it is the process of questioning that has the most value.
>
> As a staff developer, it is important for me to share the protocol related to an essential aspect of teacher practice, to question and search for answers about how teachers' practices affect student learning. However, what I am also accomplishing is modeling for my colleagues what that journey of questioning might look like. An important outcome of my research, then, is to inspire others to embark on their own road of inquiry.
>
> May we all continue to seek knowledge and forever enjoy the quest.

Although individual, collaborative, and school-based inquiry leaves us with more questions than answers, its benefits far outweigh the uncomfortable dissonance it often produces. Such benefits include changes in our beliefs, improved teaching and assessment practices, greater awareness of students' learning needs, and increased self-efficacy.

HOW CAN SCHOOLS SUPPORT INDIVIDUAL, COLLABORATIVE, AND SCHOOL-BASED RESEARCH?

Action research and systematic inquiry will emerge from a school climate that promotes the pursuit of questions of significance. Just as teachers can create a climate on inquiry in their classrooms by problematizing the curriculum, administrators, teachers, and professional developers can promote inquiry by problematizing teaching and learning. Introducing the use of essential questions such as "What are the non-negotiables of teaching and learning?" or "How do we promote excellence and equity in the classroom?" in faculty or grade-level meetings can begin the process of generating subquestions that can be the focus of individual, collaborative, or school-based inquiry. Other launching points for action research questions may come from teachers' specific problems, issues, or confusions related to their teaching, students' learning, or the curriculum and assessment products used.

Once teachers have begun the inquiry process, it is important to create collective forums where they can share their methodologies, share data, troubleshoot confusing data, analyze and discuss findings, and raise new questions for further inquiry. These forums can be created by inviting teachers who have similar interests or questions to work together or by promoting the use of inservice programs within the school focused on research and inquiry.

A good part of helping teachers come to terms with the uncertainties of action research comes from reminding teachers that inquiry is recursive and that the pursuit of a question often leads to as many new questions as answers. Often teachers find that in their pursuit of the answer to a question, confounding data or mixed findings often lead them to reframe their original question and to fine-tune or create new data collection instruments. Treating such adjustments as evidence that the teacher is making significant progress in his or her deeper understanding of a question or issue is one effective strategy in promoting ongoing inquiry.

Creating a culture of inquiry is essential to the development of a community of learners and to the cultivation of leadership. There is increasing evidence (Kouzes & Posner, 1999) that the most powerful professional development opportunities are those in which teachers are treated as scholars (producers of their own knowledge) who participate in some sort of learning community where their scholarship is fostered and valued.

POSSIBLE QUESTIONS FOR THE READER

1. What kind of inquiry, if any, is valued in your school?

2. Who conducts inquiry?

3. What is its focus?

4. How is that inquiry shared or discussed among faculty?

5. What incentives exist for individual, collaborative, or school-based inquiry?

6. What strategies could you use to support inquiry in your school?

RECOMMENDED BOOKS ON ACTION RESEARCH AND USE OF DATA

Bernhardt, Victoria. (1998). *Data analysis for comprehensive schoolwide improvement.* Larchmont, NY: Eye on Education.

> The purpose of this book is to help the reader to better collect, sort, and analyze school data so that he or she will learn how to use school data to truly affect schoolwide improvement and change. The writing style gives the impression that the quality of data analysis can improve over time. The author's writing is easy to understand, and she explains concepts with real-world examples. She lays out several levels or layers of data analysis and demonstrates how each school can tailor its data analysis to its needs. The book provides suggestions and potential plans for setting schoolwide "guiding principles."

Blythe, T., Allen, D., & Powell, B. S. (1999). *Looking together at student work: A companion guide to "Assessing student learning."* New York: Teachers College Press.

> This book provides a process for looking at student work as a tool for improving student learning and addressing the changes facing schools in light of educational reform. Work actually done in several schools using this approach is shared, along with step-by-step explanations of several models or protocols that can be adapted for use in individual schools. The process is designed for schools and teachers of all grade levels.

Burnaford, G., Fischer, J., & Hobsen, D. (1996). *Teachers doing research: Practical possibilities.* Mahwah, NJ: Lawrence Erlbaum Associates.

> This collection of articles about teacher research offers sections for beginners as well as for those already informed about teacher research. Its focus is practical, and it includes suggestions for how to do research and how to build a learning community of teachers supporting each other. A variety of teacher research examples are shared.

Glanz, J. (1998). *Action research: An educational leader's guide to school improvement.* Norwood, MA: Christopher-Gordon.

> This book provides background on educational research and a variety of ways to use action research in an educational setting. The purpose of action research, as described, is to guide decision making and planning. The steps necessary for carrying out action research are reviewed in a "user-friendly" fashion. Exercises and prompts throughout help the reader reflect on the information and think about application of the models described. The examples provided are helpful. The program and evaluation chapter details steps to follow when implementing new programs or evaluating existing ones. The realities of day-to-day decisions, deadlines for decisions that come too quickly, and the need for a better model are discussed in detail. Although the text would be helpful to individuals who want to use action research, it would be best used with a committee or a study group. The readability and strategies for action research in a meaningful context make this a valuable resource and reference.

Noffke, S. E., & Stevenson, R. B. (1995). *Educational action research: Becoming practically critical.* New York: Teachers College Press.

> This collection of essays offers a multitude of perspectives on action research. It provides thought-provoking detail and diversity, tapping into the experiences of teachers, student teachers, staff developers, principals, and others, and it focuses on the value of action research as part of school improvement. Divided into three main parts, "Action Research in Teacher Education," "Action Research in Schools," and "Supporting Action Research," the book invites readers to examine the potential, the problems, and the impact of action research in education.

Wahlstrom, D. 1999. *Using data to improve student achievement.* Virginia Beach, VA: Successline Inc.

The author has extracted a core of essential information and practice from the complex and often intimidating world of statistics, enabling uninitiated teachers and educational administrators to use data effectively as a tool for educational improvement. She gently but enthusiastically guides the novice through explanations and examples of data collection, organization, analysis, and application in schools. In the process, data begin to seem almost user friendly—more like an ally than an enemy lurking in numerical disguise! This book is full of graphics, charts, and templates that provide tools for immediate use and suggest numerous ways of understanding the cause-and-effect relationships that result in a school's statistical profile. It is a wonderful resource for any school person who needs a clear and accessible "translation" of data as a tool for examining student achievement and school change.

Professional Portfolios

4

Standards-based design and systematic inquiry demonstrate the professional expertise of teachers and administrators, yet schools seldom encourage broad dissemination of results. Too often, the authors of such projects are left without a forum to discuss, refine, or even share them. What is most important about these products and results is the process that the authors go through to develop them, the decisions made along the way, and the ways in which these products and results affect their views of their role or their understanding of teaching and learning—and that information should be made available to other teachers and administrators.

Professional portfolios are purposeful collections of work that document their authors' growth, achievements, and/or effort. They are also powerful tools for reflective practice in that they force educators to revisit decisions and actions that otherwise would remain unexamined (Martin-Kniep, 1999). When teachers and administrators select, compile, and annotate the work they place in portfolios, they document and disseminate their design and implementation of educational ideas, products, and practices. In short, portfolios reveal our professional expertise through our belief statements and reflections, our curriculum designs and products, and our description of the processes that led to our products and beliefs.

When portfolios have an audience, they become a means by which the wisdom of practice can be acknowledged and legitimated. The audience for portfolios is growing every year. Teachers and administrators are now using portfolios to seek a position, to demonstrate readiness to receive tenure, or as tools for analysis in the context of a collegial circle, study group, or action research endeavor. Teachers are required to produce a portfolio to fulfill National Board of Teacher Certification requirements, to become certified in the Center for the Study of Expertise in Teaching and Learning, and, increasingly, as part of an application process.

This chapter addresses the question: How can we use professional portfolios as frameworks for documenting professional expertise? Its major premise is that when portfolios are used to document as well as share knowledge, thinking processes, and accomplishments, they can provide a means for substantiating professional decisions, goals, and questions that often remain hidden or unrecognized. This evidence can help portfolio authors to better understand their present set of circumstances, issues, and decisions. It can also be used to capture the wisdom of expertise and to help less experienced teachers and administrators understand their own school.

WHAT DO PROFESSIONAL PORTFOLIOS INCLUDE?

Portfolios include a selection of artifacts or work samples aimed at demonstrating growth or achievement in one or more areas or outcomes. Both artifacts and outcomes reflect the diversity of teachers' and administrators' work.

Outcomes can be extraordinarily varied. They can be centered on the design and use of curriculum and assessment; the use of communication, organizational, collaborative, or management skills; the use of technology or other media; or the development and use of an educational vision or philosophy of teaching and learning.

Artifacts can also be varied. They may include units or lessons; assessments or videos of classroom activities; letters from parents, teachers, or colleagues; philosophy statements, and all kinds of reflective entries. They can also assume many different forms, such as text, photographs, and media.

To illustrate the richness of portfolios, I have selected a variety of portfolio entries that document two different outcomes, which have already been covered in this book.[1] These are (a) understanding and use of standards-based and learner-centered curriculum and assessment; and (b) use of reflection and data to improve upon own practice. The authors have used their portfolios to document the processes and products of their learning and to demonstrate proficiency or excellence in attaining the preceding outcomes. To guide them in their portfolio development process, they have used the rubric shown in Table 4.1.

UNDERSTANDING AND USE OF STANDARDS-BASED AND LEARNER-CENTERED CURRICULUM AND ASSESSMENT

Teachers and administrators provide evidence of this outcome with showcase artifacts— that is, samples of excellent work—or with growth artifacts—that is, a comparison of an original product with an improved version. Showcase artifacts can be presented in different ways and may include lessons or unit excerpts coupled with results of student work and its analysis. Table 4.2 includes two examples of student work responding to the essential question that supported a ninth-grade integrated social studies and language arts unit on Native Americans. The essential question was: "Are we really free?" In her reflection and analysis, the author asserts the validity of this artifact as an integrated, standards-based learning experience and explains how these student samples demonstrate the use of critical thinking.

Another example of a showcase artifact aimed at demonstrating specific aspects of rigorous, standards-based, and meaningful integrated curriculum is provided in Table 4.3, which shows one author's description and analysis of the key features in a secondary standards-based and process-based unit aimed at helping students engage meaningfully with a variety of literature.

A third example of a showcase piece around the design of learning opportunities is provided in Table 4.4, which depicts a study skills unit for fifth grade. Notice the use of multiple frames to simultaneously depict the artifact, contextualize it, and highlight its features.

Table 4.1   Outcomes-Based Rubric for CSETL Certification Portfolio

Dimension	Resident Fellowship Candidate	Meets Certification Requirements	Developed but Needs Revision	Emerging
Understands and can use learner-centered curriculum and assessment	Portfolio includes varied and impressive samples of student-centered curriculum that – Are inquiry based, rigorous, standards based, meaningful, and integrated in more than one way – Demand critical thinking through use of essential and guiding questions and inductive and deductive reasoning about real problems – Embed diversified diagnostic, formative, and summative assessments and authentic products and performances that measure application and knowledge throughout the learning process – Involve students in the development and use of standards-based criteria in checklists and rubrics – Provide ongoing and varied opportunities for student reflection, self-assessment, and revision	Portfolio includes varied samples of student-centered curriculum that – Are standards based, meaningful, and interdisciplinary – Demand higher-order thinking through the use of application and/or open-ended questions – Include varied diagnostic and summative assessments, products, and performances as well as recall-based tests – Use standards-based criteria in teacher-developed checklists and rubrics – Provide students with the opportunity to reflect and self-assess at the beginning and end of the learning process	Portfolio includes samples of curriculum that – Are standards based and focus on a single discipline or on parallel disciplines – Require recall, comprehension, and factual knowledge acquisition through the use of open and close-ended questions – Include limited summative products and performances as well as recall-based tests – Use explicit criteria in checklists and rubrics – Provide students with the opportunity to self- or peer-assess at some point in the learning process	Portfolio includes samples of curriculum that – Are not directly connected to standards or focus primarily on skills within a single discipline – Focus on recall of isolated knowledge, skills, and/or facts through the use of close-ended questions – Rely on traditional, recall-based tests as primary means of assessment – Lack explicit performance criteria – Preclude student reflection and self-assessment.

(Continued)

Table 4.1 (Continued)

Dimension	Resident Fellowship Candidate	Meets Certification Requirements	Developed but Needs Revision	Emerging
Uses reflection to improve upon practice	Portfolio includes varied, insightful and reflective documents/artifacts that reveal – Thorough and systematic analysis of process and meaning of own work – Accurate use of data to draw conclusions, make decisions, set goals, and generate questions for study – Identification of specific strengths and areas for improvement, supported with perceptive references to own work – Descriptions of specific strategies for improving areas in need – Setting and monitoring of both short- and long-term goals in ways that are likely to measure changes in attainment or expertise	Portfolio includes reflective documents/artifacts that reveal – Systematic analysis of value and process of own work – Accurate use of data to draw conclusions and make decisions related to own work – Identification of strengths and areas for improvement, supported with specific references to own work – Explanation of possible strategies for improving areas in need – Setting and monitoring of realistic short-term goals or of a long-term goal with accompanying supporting benchmarks	Portfolio includes reflective documents/artifacts that reveal – General analysis of meaning or quality of own work – A collection of data with no analysis or purposeful connection to own work – Identification of general strengths and areas for improvement without tangible supporting documentation – Outline of general plan for improving areas in need – Setting of realistic short-term goals that may not be directly related to or supported by work	Portfolio includes descriptive documents/artifacts that reveal – The kind of work done – Data missing, misrepresented, or irrelevant to work included – Description of process and struggles related to work without supporting documents – Plan for improvements sketchy or missing – General, vague statements of future goals

Growth artifacts are equally effective in demonstrating expertise. One example of a technique that illustrates growth in the ability to create rich learner-centered experiences is provided in one author's simultaneous depiction of two different tasks and analysis of the improvements made in the revised version (Table 4.5).

Another example is provided in an author's small collection of samples aimed at showing growth in the ability to design standards-based units. These samples include an introductory analysis of a project-based unit developed years ago, followed by annotations of the changes

Table 4.2   Snapshots of Work Accomplished

EXCERPT FROM JOSH'S DBQ ESSAY	EXCERPT FROM NEAL'S DBQ ESSAY
Essential Question: Are we really free? **Guiding Question:** What forces have limited freedom for Native Americans?	**Essential Question:** Are we really free? **Guiding Question:** What forces have promoted freedom for Native Americans?
Thesis Statement:	**Thesis Statement and First Paragraph:**
In the history of the Native Americans, the settlers made them work until the Indians were dead. The settlers limited the Native Americans freedom by doing that. This can be proven by the historical documents in history. Las Casas showed the cruelty the Native Americans were getting. Corn Tassel showed the numbers of the settlers far exceeded the number of the Native Americans and it showed the Indians had no fighting chance to save their land. <u>The Act to Regulate Trade</u> limited the Indians freedom because they could not seek private revenge. All these documents have evidence from the history of the Native Americans that they haven't been acknowledged as human beings worthy of freedom.	The Native Americans were sometimes valued as people. Some Spanish and Americans promoted freedom for the Natives. Las Casas's writings about the plight of the Indians in 1552, <u>General Washington's Letter of Support</u> written in 1779, and the <u>Declaration of Indian Purpose</u> of 1961 give evidence that freedom was supported for the Indians. Las Casas was a Spaniard that thought that Indian slavery was wrong and wrote a document called La Casas and the plight of the Indians. Las Casas was agents the harsh labor that the Indians had suffered. They were put to work in the mines were they dug gold for melting. The Indians starved and died. His letter helped stop Indian slavery in the 1550's. Las Casas was called the ARCHENEMY OF SPAIN.

REFLECTION and ANALYSIS

What I think is powerful from these excerpts is that both students used the same document as evidence for opposing sides of the essential question. Josh interprets the abuse of the Indians as evidence for limiting their freedom, whereas Neal cites the letter documenting the abuse as evidence that freedom was in fact supported.

Josh has a well developed and well organized thesis that was developed with the thesis planning sheet I created along with the outline. I think his last sentence provides evidence of his insight. His essay has developed paragraphs using all the information that was documented in the early stages of unpacking the texts. Neal's style is more succinct. When Josh, Neal and I rated Neal's essay individually using my general writing rubric, we all rated the essay exactly the same!

Curriculum and Assessment:
  A.   are inquiry based, rigorous standards-based, meaningful and integrated in more than one way
  B.   demand critical thinking through the use of essential and guiding questions and inductive and deductive reasoning

Table 4.3   Description and Analysis of a Curriculum Unit

This prototype describes a learning activity that meets all of the English Language Arts Standards and uses all four of the modalities: reading, writing, listening, and speaking. Since students select the materials they will present from their independent reading, students often make selections that make interdisciplinary connections. Sometimes students choose biographical material that emerges from social studies themes. Students often refer to lessons they have learned in health when they choose selections that relate to self-esteem. Students have focused on science issues and have shown how that discipline relies on language use. Since the choice of the topic depends on the student's personal connection, any discipline or genre may be used in creating a GROUP SHARE.

Table 4.4 Designing Learning Opportunities

Writing Project	Year/Writers	Summary	Reflection
Study Skills: Grade 5	1997: Barbara A. Colton & Dr. Michelle Pessin-Brill, Inclusive Special Ed., Ph.D.—Learning Styles	Study Skills Model: intermediate grades Unit 1: Self-Assessment Unit 2: Self-Esteem Unit 3: Environment	Michelle and I were the Grade 5 inclusion team. She specialized in learning and I brought curriculum expertise. We focused on self-exploration. Outcome: a user-friendly interactive self-awareness model teaching study skills/learning styles/multiple intelligences.

Learning Skills: MORE ABOUT ME
A Course of Study
Dr. Pessin-Brill and Ms. Colton

Units of Study	Lesson Plan	Follow-up
I. Self-Assessment	1. Getting to Know Yourself	World Map
	2. Learning About Me	
	3. Learning From Our Mistakes	
	4. Healthy Snacks	One-Day Food List
	5. Relaxation	
	Culminating Activity	
II. Self-Esteem	1. Getting Acquainted	You Are Wonderful
	2. Cheer Yourself Up	
	3. Gratitude Journal	Gratitude Journal
	4. Smile Memoir	
	Culminating Activity	
III. Environment	1. Getting Organized	My Room
	2. Home Environment	
	3. Time Juggling	Schedule
	4. Prioritize	To Do List
	Culminating Activity	

Summary (continued):

Name: _____

Getting to Know Yourself Checklist

It is important to know yourself and what things affect you. Once you have identified what you find difficult, you will be better able to come up with plans to overcome these difficulties.
Put an X next to any of the following sentences that describe you or your behavior.

§ It is hard for me to pay attention to my teacher when he/she is talking.
§ When I should be working I am often thinking of other things.
§ I have trouble starting my work.
§ I have trouble finishing my work.
§ I am disorganized.
§ I have trouble sitting still.
§ I have trouble making or keeping friends.
§ I have trouble following rules.
§ I forget what I am supposed to do.
§ It is hard for me to get ready for school on time in the morning.
§ Noises or other children in the classroom distract me.
§ I frequently lose things.

Study Tip: When you know yourself, you will be able to communicate your needs more clearly to others.

Reflection (continued):

Name: _____

Time Juggling

Are you an efficient juggler? Can you manage the time that you have effectively? This activity will help you examine how well you are budgeting your time. Using the attached sheet:

1. Write your daily after-school activities for the week. Music lessons, sports, play dates, appointments, talking on the phone, watching TV.
2. Draw a box around the remaining empty time, spaces. These are the hours that you are free to do school work and study. For each day add the number of hours that you have *free time*. Record that number in the free time box for that day.
3. During the week, record daily how much time you spent doing school work or studying. Record that number in the study time box for that day.

Review the findings of your time spent over the past week.
1. Did you have enough time to study? _____
2. Did you have enough time to do your homework carefully and completely? _____
3. Did you have enough time to participate in after school activities? _____

If your answer was YES to all three questions—you are a TIME JUGGLER. If you answered NO to any of the questions, look again at your schedule to see how you can make changes.
Study Tip: Time management is a life skill. We all must prioritize and make conscious choices in life. More time to study might mean less time watching TV or talking on the phone.

Unit tables of contents evidences focus on the self in three modules.	Self-awareness checklist used to promote self- and group discovery.	Prioritizing time management as a factor in reducing stress.

Table 4.5   Depiction of Two Tasks and Analysis

The revised Constellation Project, written in Spring 2000, shows the subtle but important change that has occurred in my concept of what a good curriculum unit looks like. The revised assessment is focused on the essential question that ties the whole curriculum together: "What is our place in the universe?" The new curriculum and assessment unit is well grounded within the development sequence of the course, is tied to the other tasks through the essential question, and has a real audience and purpose; the student presentations are spread out through the semester and serve as minilessons that introduce the phenomena that lead to an understanding of the structure and/or nature of the universe.

ORIGINAL TASK	REVISED TASK
In this project you will investigate a constellation that is visible in the Northern Hemisphere. You will present your findings in class in a 5- to 10-minute talk with questions afterward. For your presentation you should: • Prepare a pamphlet which you will distribute to the class • Select laser disk pictures and slides to illustrate your talk • Create a visual display which shows what your constellation looks like • Select three important facts that everyone should know about your constellation—test questions will come from these statements	**Essential Question:** What is our place in the universe? **Guiding Questions for the Constellation Project:** • What does this constellation look like? • How can we find it in the sky? (time/season, star hop, celestial coordinates, etc.) • What ancient stories were told about this grouping of stars? • How does the story connect the constellation to others in the sky? • What deep space objects lie in this region? How do they help us to understand the universe (structure, age, evolution, etc.) **Task:** In this project you will investigate a constellation that is visible in the Northern Hemisphere. Throughout the year you will present your findings to the class in a 5- to 10-minute talk, with the opportunity for everyone to ask questions afterwards. The presentations will be scheduled to fit with our inquiry as we investigate our place in the universe. • Prepare a **pamphlet** which you will distribute to the class • Prepare a **presentation that includes visual displays** which shows what your constellation looks like and pictures of some of the unusual objects that can be seen • Select **three important facts** that everyone should know about your constellation—test questions will come from these statements

made to improve it (Table 4.6). To support this analysis, the author included additional documents, such as a synopsis of the original project as students would receive it, a checklist that guides students' self-assessment of the revised project, a list of standards and performance indicators that are measured in the revised project, and photographs of students sharing their final work.

Table 4.6   Continuing on the Path Toward a Well-Developed Unit: A Reflection

The original scale model unit was developed to give seventh- and eighth-grade students who have emotional and learning challenges a hands-on experience that integrated work with decimals, fractions, and proportional relationships. Following are the revisions I have made on the unit based on my recent exposure to standards-based design.

List the standards that are addressed in the project and design rubrics based on the standards: In the original unit, I was aware of the standards that I was addressing but did not make the students aware of the standards.

Allow students choice: In the original unit, all students built a scale model of the classroom. In the redesigned unit, students choose the space they will construct.

Make sure that there is a real purpose for the task: In the original unit there was not a real-life purpose for the task. In the redesigned unit, students will implement the classroom design that best meets the needs of the group (the students will determine which design that is); students who design a model of the room in their home will take before and after pictures. The before picture will be an actual picture of the room and after will be a picture of either the scale model or the newly designed space. Some students may choose to build a dollhouse that is a scale model of their home. The dollhouse could be donated to a preschool classroom.

Develop a rubric for each portion of the project rather than utilizing one rubric for the entire task: The original unit relied on one rubric to evaluate the entire task. The rubric was not specific enough. Utilizing a rubric for each portion of the task will allow students to focus on each portion of the task and prevent them from making errors in next steps because of an error in a previous step.

Incorporate career awareness via interviews with professionals who use two- and three-dimensional models in their work: There was no specific link to careers in the original unit. Talking with professionals who utilize the skills that the students are learning will allow students to see a real application and purpose for the tasks they are asked to complete.

I am planning to pilot the unit with students in a new alternative middle school, which I am helping to develop. I am eager to compare the student work from this unit to the student work from the previous unit and to get feedback on the revisions from students and teachers.

USE OF REFLECTION AND DATA TO IMPROVE ONE'S PRACTICE

Without a strong reflective component, portfolios serve primarily as measures of our professional competence. When accompanied by an ongoing and explicit reflective process, portfolios are windows into the processes and the means by which we shape, question, and refine our professional identities. The reflective component of professional portfolios includes but is not limited to an analysis of the strengths and weaknesses in our work, often accompanied by a statement on how we intend to maximize our strengths and minimize our shortcomings; the articulation of our professional goals with accompanying strategies and timelines for attaining them; an analysis of the extent to which our activities and strategies are helping us address our goals; our belief system in the form of vision statements, educational philosophies, or educational platforms, with accompanying evidence of the work that embodies our beliefs; and the articulation of questions or issues that affect our thinking, with a supporting action plan for addressing these.

The reflective component transforms showcase documents into learning devices for teachers, administrators, and ultimately for students. According to Stronge (2002), "Teachers whose students have high achievement rates continually mention reflection on

Table 4.7   Three Excerpts From "Dear Reader" Letters

Excerpt 1

"What sparks learning?" is an essential question that drives my work as an educator. . . . I love to learn and that passion for learning is what I want to transmit to my students and colleagues. This love spans a wide spectrum: from learning about the Earth and investigating what provokes an ongoing enjoyment of exploring new ideas, to making a decent chip shot and getting the roses to grow organically without black spot. Who I am is what I do. Learning is the spark that fuels my life, and I want to share it with others.

In this portfolio you will find a small collection of work that shows what I have been learning about the sparks of learning in several areas: teaching science, working as a staff developer, writing curriculum, and my experience as a lifelong learner. The quest to find that elusive recipe for what sparks learning, the so what, is underway. The following pages will give a glimpse of my journey along that path.

Excerpt 2

People who know me find it completely inconsistent that I have been an avid follower of the Survivor series since I am not one who generally watches television for entertainment nor one who relishes group-bonding experiences. Yet one might draw some parallels to participation in CSETL with the Survivor genre since each new Fellow has to establish his or her own identity and learn the ropes to survive. . . .

I had begun work on this portfolio and was searching for its unifying thread. The Survivor metaphor represents the quest for self-discovery through collaboration.

Excerpt 3

Here is my portfolio, an interactive briefcase, whose contents will, I hope, reflect my development from classroom teacher to staff developer.

As you look through the briefcase, you will find one computer disk and several file folders. On disk is the narrative or my journey, annotated to indicate supporting artifacts and/or documents which can be found in the folders.

The *Itinerary* outlines the layout and establishes the color-coding that will help you navigate from one part to another, and back again if you so choose.

their work as an important part of improving their teaching. Belief in one's efficacy and maintaining high expectations for students are common among teachers who reflect" (p. 21).

The first reflective portfolio entry, and perhaps most important artifact, is the "dear reader" letter. This letter introduces the portfolio as a collection and makes explicit its purpose and design. The excerpts from three different letters in Table 4.7 illustrate their use of reflection and their value in helping readers "get into" the portfolios. The first excerpt introduces the question that drives this portfolio and links it to the artifacts included. The second excerpt introduces and explains the portfolio's motif. The last excerpt describes the structure that houses the author's portfolio.

Educational platforms constitute another important reflective entry included in many portfolios. They are statements that articulate the beliefs of teachers and educational leaders (Combs et al., 1999). Once they are made, their authors can use them to make decisions and revisit them for future decision making and action. Sergiovanni and Starratt (1979) advocate articulating beliefs about such matters as the aims of education, major achievements desired of students, the social significance of student learning, images of the learner, the value of the curriculum, and the purposes of supervision. Table 4.8 provides two examples of educational platforms found in professional portfolios.

Portfolios can include additional reflective artifacts to analyze growth and attainment or to set goals and make decisions. One example of how the reflective use of data can be used to

Table 4.8   Two Educational Platforms

Example 1

The evolution of life and learning happens as we pursue the quality of those things that are relevant and important to our journey. As a result of my inquiry regarding the differences between adults and children in terms of their learning needs, I realize that there is no real difference between educators and our students in the way we move and learn from a new experience.

Example 2

   I believe that before teachers and administrators can build a vision on student learning, the ability to be a reflective practitioner is essential. I think the use of reflection as is defined for teachers in my school is part of the process of building a shared vision. It is how we dialogue about specific aspects of teaching. It is how we "do things for each other."

   The direct connection with what teachers say and how we move forward based on the content and my analysis of what they say is integrated in all of my work with teachers. Reflection and feedback on learning and needs slowly become part of the school culture.

Table 4.9   Analysis of Laboratory Experiment

Since the 1999–2000 school year I have been exploring ways to help students think critically. . . . My goal has been to facilitate student understanding of their lab work by helping them to approach the analysis and synthesis of the data. . . . The lab books that we use have a series of analysis questions followed by a conclusion question that serves as a summary. My experience has been that students can answer the analysis questions, often without doing or understanding the lab work, and can write a conclusion statement by rewording the introduction and/or purpose of the lab.

   I have refocused my expectations for what students do, and have been working out ways for students to make sense of the process of science throughout the year.

The process has included many different strategies, such as:

- Redefining the purpose of the conclusion. I revamped the conclusion so that students no longer gave a brief response but used it to prove that they understood the activity by citing data to support their statements and making connections to activities or events outside the lab experience.
- Designing a lab conclusion rubric to align the new conclusion purpose and support mathematics, science and technology standards as well as English language arts standards.
- Creating an activity where students analyze a model conclusion to determine how the scaffolded lab analysis questions can be used to help write the conclusions.
- Constructing a prewriting graphic organizer.
- Setting up rewriting groups so students would write the conclusion in a jigsaw—the lab group would brainstorm and the rewrite group would prewrite the conclusion using a graphic organizer.
- Encouraging students to rewrite a conclusion by allowing them to improve their grade on two labs at the end of the quarter.

---

improve upon one's practice is included in a portfolio section where the author analyzes her use of laboratory experiments (Table 4.9). To illustrate the effect of the changes made to the labs in her classes, this author included work from one of her students, showing the changes in the articulation and specificity of her lab conclusions over a few months.

   Two more examples of the use of reflection to improve one's teaching so as to enhance students' learning are found in the entries shown in Table 4.10. The first example shows reflection on a particular classroom exercise; the second shows reflection on the author's general strengths and weaknesses in teaching, underscoring his self-awareness and desire to minimize his shortcomings.

   Professional portfolios often include a reflective section where the author identifies needs and sets new goals based on his or her analysis of the work included. Table 4.11 shows several examples of these goal statements. The first one is rather general, whereas the second two are more specific. In general, the more specific the goal and strategy statements, the easier it is to monitor their attainment.

Table 4.10 Two Examples of the Use of Reflection to Improve One's Teaching

Example 1

The debates were excellent. Students used their time wisely researching and preparing. . . . Originally, I had set time limits of 20 minutes for each debate. At their request, I allowed students to exceed this time limit. This resulted in debates that lasted an entire class period. . . . Although it was reassuring to see the wealth of information gathered by each group, it was a mistake to give students unlimited time for their debates because the audience attentiveness was compromised. Students also missed out on the opportunity to prioritize and condense information into summaries. I have decided that next year debates will be timed, with a maximum of 25 minutes, allowing for two debates per period. Students will have one minute each for an opening and a closing, and ten minutes to present arguments and rebuttals. Reading will be kept to a minimum and information will be streamlined. I'll amend the debate assessment checklist to help students prioritize and synthesize information.

Example 2

Being willing to engage in process-oriented learning has been my strength as a teacher, along with a desire to seek out mentors from whom I can grow and develop. I'm also a hard worker and fairly creative. As a risk taker, I will readily implement new ideas and strategies that I find worthwhile into my teaching, even when I find the process messy, confusing, and difficult at first. I prefer rich, interdisciplinary experiences for my students, and I have taken the initiative to develop several learning opportunities which reflect these qualities.

My weaknesses include that I am not as effective at teaching students on the lower end of the spectrum, becoming frustrated with my ability to influence students whose emotional problems cause disinterest in learning, and parents who seek to manage my teaching or classroom practices in accordance with their own set of expectations. As a learner, I have high standards which can also cause me to become stressed and overwhelmed during those times when I feel my work is not yet good enough. I am trying to learn to manage these tendencies.

Table 4.11 Three Needs and Goals Statements

Example 1

As I continue to reflect on my needs, I recognize that I cannot do "everything" within a given theme or concept, I need to use ongoing assessments to structure lessons. I need to follow up on areas of need more consistently before moving on to new topics. I need to use self-assessments more effectively so my students may realize the impact they can have on their learning processes.

Example 2

I want to work on capturing and measuring the impact that staff development has upon teachers' instructional practices and student achievement. . . . I would like to look at three different staff development formats: online courses, short-term programs (1–3 days); and long-term programs (1–3 years).

I would also like to either develop a primary level prototype to be field-tested by a group of teachers from the Genesee Valley BOCES region, or field-test an existing CSETL prototype with a group of teachers from that region. In either case, I will serve as a group facilitator in the analysis and modifications of the prototype.

Example 3

As I look on the work that I have done so far I find that there are several areas to work on. In the past I have consistently used teacher-generated rubrics; students have had the opportunity for revision on occasion but have rarely availed themselves of this, and I have not pushed the issue; this year I would like to have students use exemplars and models to create the rubrics for themselves and then use them more consistently for revision. . . .

Although I have used diagnostics, particularly in the beginning of the year to set up lab groups and provide a benchmark against which students can measure their growth, I would like to use them in a different way. I would like to design a few differentiated tasks and match the task with the students based on the diagnostic.

HOW ARE PROFESSIONAL PORTFOLIOS ORGANIZED?

Professional portfolios can be as varied in their form and packaging as the authors who develop them. They can be packaged in binders; in briefcases with multiple zippers, each one containing a chapter or section; in Web sites or CD-ROMs; or in interconnected artistic panels that juxtapose image and text. Figure 4.1 includes three examples.

The external packaging of portfolios frequently features a variety of organizational frameworks that support the portfolio's contents. Portfolios can be structured around a

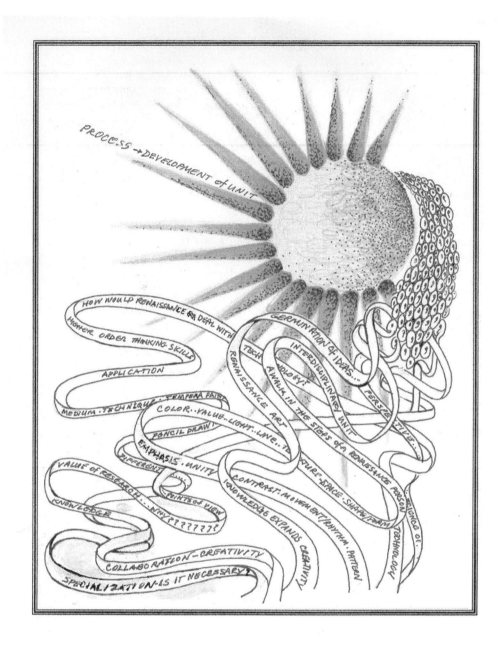

Figure 4.1   Three Images of Professional Portfolios (*Continued*)

theme, such as "The Road Not Taken" or "Where did I come from? Where am I now? Where am I going?" They can also be centered on an image (photograph of a labyrinth), a motif or metaphor ("Survivor," "Portfolio as Yeast"), or a question ("What Sparks Learning?").

These diverse frameworks are representative of the learning preferences and writing styles of different authors. Figure 4.2 and Table 4.12 show two very different frameworks. The first was developed by a visual learner who uses imagery as an organizational tool. The second was developed by an author who thinks in a linear and logical fashion and who uses a sequential organizational structure. This structure permeates her "Dear Reader" letter.

Figure 4.1   (Continued)

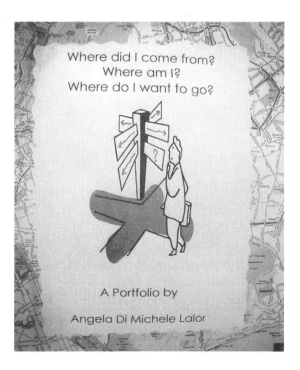

Portfolios can even have a fluid and recursive structure, such as that provided by a Web site. Figure 4.3 shows the home page of an actual Web-based portfolio.

Finding a framework or a metaphor to house one's portfolio is, in and of itself, an introspective and creative task. After all, how many times in our lives are we compelled to

Figure 4.2   A Portfolio Framework Developed by a Visual Learner

My Journey Through the Labyrinth: Visions of My Learning

Section One The Learner		
Labyrinth Journey	*Through My Lens*	*Teaching Analogy*
As I approached the labyrinth I was fascinated with its form. . . . It was inviting and intriguing in the same breath. And so I entered. . . . Life is a wonderful adventure. Inside the labyrinth one's perspective changes. The path before you becomes unclear. The journey that from the outside seemed so clear was suddenly unsettling.		When I entered the teaching profession I was eager to teach. What I realize today, I was eager to pass on what I learned in college to the students in my classroom. I was the keeper of the keys of knowledge. Everything was so clear and simple. I remember saying to a mother of 6, "Just find the time to read with Patrick for 10 minutes each night." When I became a parent of 3 I realized how complex a day becomes for both mother and child. I learned not to judge.

Section One Artifacts:
- "Dear Reader" Letter
- Resume

This section of the portfolio paints a picture of Barbara A. Colton the learner. Self-reflection sets the tone of the portfolio.

Table 4.12   A "Dear Reader" Entry Using a Linear, Logical Style

Where did I come from? Where am I? Where do I want to go? In order to best capture my travels as an educator, I have used these questions to frame my portfolio. The "Dear Reader" letter serves as the overview of the portfolio. It provides a summary of the sections and an introduction to the component parts. Each section includes an analysis of the samples presented and their connection to the portfolio outcomes. The portfolio closes with a description of what I have learned by completing the portfolio, identifying my strengths, needs, and appropriate next steps, followed by my concluding remarks.

represent ourselves through artifacts and images that speak for us? Most teachers and administrators begin the search for this framework by identifying the outcomes they want to target and then matching those outcomes with one or more artifacts to use as evidence of their attainment.

One of the trademarks of a well-developed portfolio is the clarity and congruence of the linkage between portfolio outcomes and artifacts (Martin-Kniep, 1999). Table 4.13 shows two strategies for establishing the relationship between outcomes and artifacts. The first

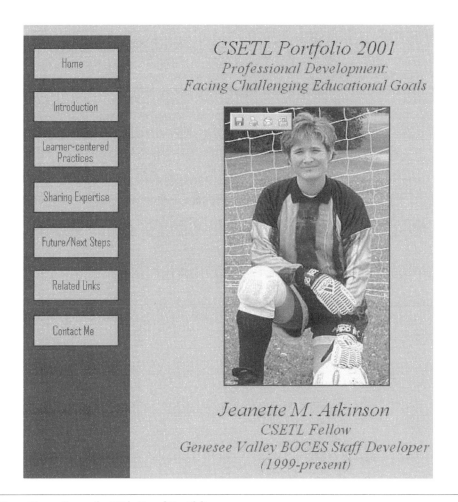

Figure 4.3   Home Page of a Web-Based Portfolio

strategy links specific outcomes with artifacts. The second strategy articulates the specific relationship between outcomes, indicators, and artifacts and explicitly describes the evidence in the artifacts that validates the indicators.

Perhaps the most significant challenge faced by many portfolio developers is deciding how much or how little to use as evidence. This is especially true when there is an outside audience for the portfolio that serves as a reader, critical friend, or evaluator. Finding the true essence of one's work requires that we distance ourselves from our products and efforts and find sections or excerpts that clearly exemplify an outcome or validate an assertion.

The difficulty of organizing the artifacts into a coherent product that represents and speaks for the author as a professional is exacerbated by shifts in professional roles and responsibilities. The entry shown in Table 4.14 captures this challenge.

Whereas one could easily say that portfolios are never finished in that they represent our present and sometimes past view of ourselves and our work, there is something deeply satisfying in completing and showcasing a portfolio, and the process is valuable for increasing self-understanding. This is artfully captured in the two entries shown in Table 4.15.

The development of a professional portfolio can provide many benefits to teachers and administrators, including

Table 4.13   Two Strategies: Outcomes and Artifacts

Strategy 1

Portfolio Sample	Portfolio Outcome
Classroom outcomes	Understands and can use learner-centered curriculum and assessment
	Uses reflection to improve upon practice
"My Personal Connection" prototype	Understands and can use learner-centered curriculum and assessment
	Uses reflection to improve upon practice
	Demonstrates the ability to present oneself as a professional
"Rubric on Rubrics"	Demonstrates a commitment to share expertise

Strategy 2
Outcome: Understands and Can Use Learner-Centered Curriculum and Assessment

Indicator	Artifact	Evidence
Inquiry based, rigorous, standards based, integrated, and meaningful	"Quiet Garden" prototype	Academic rigor via analysis and use of data
		Integration of language arts, economics, geography, mathematics, science, and career development standards
		Student-designed experiments drive task (design of a garden pond)
		Applying new knowledge in presentation for an audience gives project purpose and meaning

Table 4.14   Challenge of Self-Definition

This portfolio has been a "work in non-progress" for about 2 years now. It has existed in bits and pieces on disks and hard drives, in piles in my head and in my house. It has been a source of frustration and a goal—what I have openly said is a priority, yet what I have been most successful in avoiding.

I was unable to find a "framework" that fit, unable to identify a "type" of portfolio, unable to tease out the story to be told or to even find the voice with which to tell it. It was a strange and uncomfortable experience, this inability to communicate.

Looking back over these past years, I see, I think, that the reason for all of these difficulties had more to do with the rapid rate of changes I was undergoing than with some inability to verbalize in more than self-absorbed, adolescent meanderings.

Table 4.15   Two Entries on Portfolios and Understanding

Example 1

The process of creating this portfolio has given me the opportunity to really examine what's been going on during the past two years. In sifting through the folders and presentations I've made and the projects I've facilitated, I found myself re-reading samples of teachers' work and reflections that I've saved. Not only did they serve to remind me of specific people and experiences, they provided me with evidence that what I've done hasn't always been a slick and polished production, it has always resulted in changes in participants' understanding, ability, and sometimes even their practice.

Example 2

In documenting my teaching life with my series of portfolios I have come to understand myself as a teacher. Since completing my first portfolio in 1995 I have had all my students keep portfolios, and while some years I have done a more thorough job than others, each class has benefited from their portfolio work. Keeping a portfolio demands an honest look at one's experience and the cataloguing, examining, and explaining of the process is where the learning takes place.

- Clarifying their values and beliefs
- Identifying products and processes that are most significant
- Examining professional growth and attainment
- Celebrating achievements
- Identifying and monitoring goals with strategies for accomplishing them
- Asserting their own uniqueness and individuality.

HOW CAN SCHOOLS BEGIN TO SUPPORT THE DEVELOPMENT AND USE OF PROFESSIONAL PORTFOLIOS?

One of the conditions that tends to predict whether or how professional portfolios will be developed and used over time is the presence of a real purpose and audience for the portfolio process. Legitimate purposes might include teacher induction; teacher and administrative certification and validation; and evidence of program impact.

In the area of teacher induction, administrators may want to support having new teachers develop and maintain portfolios in their first 3 years of teaching. Ideally, new teachers can be paired with experienced teachers who can help them identify the appropriate documents to demonstrate evidence of their growth and attainment as teachers. The areas of professional practice that can be documented include content knowledge, pedagogical content knowledge, knowledge and use of varied instructional strategies, knowledge and use of varied assessment approaches, ability to address the needs of diverse learners, and use of curriculum. Frameworks such as the one developed by Danielson and McGreal (2000) may be useful in determining the range and nature of the portfolio entries. These portfolios can greatly enhance current teacher evaluation practices, which are often limited by periodic observations, many of them lacking a context for making significant judgments about their validity. The use of expert teachers as legitimate mentors also creates legitimate mechanisms for the transfer and sharing of expertise among teachers, and it can support the creation of specific learning communities centered on a common goal.

In the area of teacher and administrative certification, professional portfolios can be used as a mechanism to stimulate continuous growth and to identify expertise. Many of the best practices of teachers and administrators occur in the absence of a forum to document them, and portfolios can address this problem. The development of these portfolios can be framed in the context of an alternative to traditional evaluation approaches for tenured staff. If school administrators consider identifying and supporting the national certification process for teachers, the portfolio development process is a logical first step in terms of identifying possible candidates for national certification and supporting their certification requirements. Administrators could also benefit from a collegial documentation and certification process. Their professional lives are often as fragmented as those of teachers, and they could greatly benefit from a process that helps them articulate their goals, activities, questions, and strategies.

Last, professional portfolios can be used by teachers, administrators, and staff developers to document the impact of short- and long-term school and teacher improvement processes in schools. Organizations such as the National Staff Development Council have recently articulated the need to increase the rigor of professional development and document its impact beyond participants' perceptions. The work of Bernhardt (1998) could be useful in developing school portfolios.

POSSIBLE QUESTIONS FOR THE READER

1. When and how are teachers encouraged to reflect in your school?

2. Are teachers encouraged to document their growth and attainment in any way?

3. Are teachers or administrators encouraged to compile professional portfolios?

4. How are they used or shared? Who supports this work and how?

5. If teachers or administrators compile professional portfolios, who reads them? For what purpose?

RECOMMENDED BOOKS ON PORTFOLIOS

Belanoff, P., & Dickson, M. (1991). *Portfolios: Process and product.* Portsmouth, NH: Heinemann.

This book explores different ways portfolios can be used. It is divided into three parts: "Portfolios for Proficiency Testing," "Portfolios for Program Assessment," and "Classroom Portfolios." The strength of this collection of articles and narratives is that it combines theory and research with practice and history. It also describes the range and meaning of portfolios as assessment devices.

Black, L., Daiker, D., Summers, J., & Stygall, G. (1994). *New directions in portfolio assessment.* Portsmouth, NH: Boynton/Cook.

This book provides varying views and experiences related to the use of portfolios for learning and assessment. The use of portfolios is explored from Grades K through 12, and there are some examples of portfolio use at the university level. The book is divided into three parts. "Part One: Perspectives" presents philosophical concerns on uses and purposes of portfolios in the classroom; "Part Two: Portfolios in the Classroom" includes three sections, "Student Voices," "Teacher Voices," and "Teacher Learning." The last section is "Part Three: Large-Scale Portfolio Assessment."

Burke, K. (1997). *Designing professional portfolios for change.* Arlington Heights, IL: IRI/Skylight.

This book offers a hands-on, step-by-step approach for documenting change through the use of professional portfolios. The author distinguishes between inservice, professional development, and staff development and then describes a variety of professional portfolios. Chapters are dedicated to resources, data collection, collaboration, selection and organization, reflection, evaluation, and conferences and exhibits. The book includes charts that structure various components of a portfolio and the complete portfolio of a fictitious 11th-grade English teacher.

Graves, D. H., & Sunstein, B. S. (1992). *Portfolio portraits.* Portsmouth, NH: Heinemann.

The authors have compiled a unique look at portfolios through the personal "hands-on" experiences of several educators as they grow in their understanding of the meaning and use of this new tool. Readers can gain insight into portfolios as both an evaluative and an instructional vehicle that is closely aligned to self-evaluation and literacy itself.

Green, J. E., & Smyser, S. O. (1996). *The teacher portfolio.* Lancaster, PA: Technomic Publishing.

> This text is a practical guide for teachers and administrators who want to use teaching portfolios as a strategy for professional development. Examples are given that can be used to incorporate teacher portfolios into a teacher evaluation program. The "Five I's" are presented as a guide for portfolio development: introduction, influences, instruction, individualization, and integration. These five areas are explained clearly, with teacher examples used to support and further define each focus area.

Martin-Kniep, G. O. (1998). *Why am I doing this?* Portsmouth, NH: Heinemann.

> This book is about changing teachers' practices through extensive professional development opportunities. It is about the work of more than 100 teachers in an initiative called the Hudson Valley Portfolio Assessment Project. It is divided into three sections. The first section explains the Hudson Valley Portfolio Assessment Project, the program components, and the design process to develop new forms of assessment. The second section reveals several different teacher's stories related to changing the ways they think about learning and curriculum. In the third part of this book, the author discusses the nature of teacher change. An appendix contains interesting charts, teacher evaluation rubrics, and a simulation on managing change amidst multiple interests.

Martin-Kniep, G. O. (1999). *Capturing the wisdom of practice: Professional portfolios for educators.* Alexandria, VA: Association for Supervision and Curriculum Development.

> This introductory guide has all the steps and strategies you need to create your own portfolio and help others create theirs too: (a) ways to start your portfolio and make sure it reflects your abilities and accomplishments; (b) what to include in a portfolio if you are a teacher or an administrator; (c) types of portfolios that are best for researchers, professional developers, or curriculum designers; (d) examples of effective portfolios and systemwide portfolio efforts; and (e) four areas of portfolio specialization: learner, researcher, professional developer, and curriculum and assessment developer.

NOTE

1. The entries included in this chapter were selected from portfolios developed by the following CSETL fellows: Jeanette Atkinson, Elizabeth Bedell, Lisa Boerum, Barbara Colton, Angela DiMichele Lalor, Dee Fulgione, Richard Hinrichs, Linda Hughs, Kristin Kendall-Jakus, Kathleen Perry, Joanne Picone-Zocchia, and Anne Smith. To enhance the flow and continuity in the chapter, I have omitted citing the author of each portfolio entry.

Developing
An Action Plan

In this book we have explored four different methods for developing learning communities that acknowledge and maximize upon the expertise of teachers and other educators. Following are the elements of an action plan that would enable administrators, teachers, and staff developers to operationalize these methods in their schools.

IDENTIFICATION OF INTERNAL EXPERTISE

Every school has its own pockets of expertise, but in most cases the magnitude of such expertise goes unrecognized. A beginning step for a school to develop a learning community is to identify the school's own internal capacity for staff to learn and help one another. In Chapter 1, I described the use of databases that can be compiled on a yearly basis. Gathering data on teachers' interests and passions will result in the identification of areas of expertise and will further the goal of identifying potential teams, study groups, or collegial circles. The data can be obtained through surveys or interviews of staff, through self-developed knowledge, through skills and interests profiles that staff could complete, and through information found in teachers' job applications, performance reviews, or observations.

The information-gathering and sharing process should be done in an atmosphere in which all participants know they have something important to contribute to the well-being of the school. It's also important that this data collection process be engaged in on a continuous basis to acknowledge growth in staff.

ASSESSMENT OF NEEDS

Learning communities should address the needs of teachers, students, or the school as an organization. Needs assessment processes can be done on individuals, groups of teachers, or the school as a whole. Ideally, the identification of needs should be done in the context of a grounded understanding of students' needs and performance. It is important that needs be categorized into those that can be affected by teachers or by the school and those that escape the school's influence.

Among the data that can be used prior to identifying needs are

- Students' learning data from a variety of sources, including standardized tests, school and classroom assessments, report cards, longitudinal achievement data (as available), and schoolwide documentation of student information
- Findings from shared-decision and school improvement school and district teams
- Historical data on the school and district: changing demographics, enrollment, facilities, financial trends, and administrative shifts
- Findings from teams that have visited and assessed the school
- Community survey results
- Mission, vision, and goal statements that have been generated in the school over the years

Once needs have been identified and prioritized, administrators or staff developers may consider engaging the staff in a visioning process such as the one described by DuFour and Eaker (1998). This process uses the needs assessment process as the foundation to identify and reconcile individual and school-based goals.

BROKERING OF RELATIONSHIPS AMONG TEACHERS

Administrators and professional developers are uniquely qualified to forge relationships and alliances among teachers who may otherwise not work together or even know each other. Access to individual teachers' classroom practices, interests, goals, and activities provides administrators with far deeper knowledge of individual teachers than teachers have of each other. Similarly, having the opportunity to facilitate knowledge and skills gives staff developers access to teachers' levels of understanding or use of selected concepts or practices.

Given that teaching is primarily a solitary act, administrators and professional developers can greatly enhance meaningful exchanges and collaboration among staff through cross-classroom visitation opportunities and through the development of teams, study groups, collegial circles, or action research initiatives.

The successful development of these collaborative structures requires the following conditions (DuFour & Eaker, 1998):

- Time should be built into the school program for groups to work together, review and analyze their work, discuss student learning in light of that work, and raise questions for further inquiry. Without the provision of real time for teachers to work together, it will be difficult for teachers to appreciate the truthfulness of the school's commitment to such work.
- The scope and purpose of the collaborative work should be explicit and known to everyone. As DuFour and Eaker (1998) have established, the development of teams is a means to an end and not an end in itself. It is important for all involved to understand what they are trying to accomplish, what success will look like, and what the parameters of work and responsibility entail. Ideally, the group itself should participate in the identification of goals, scope, and responsibilities.
- If there is no tradition for collaborative work among adults in the school, the teams and other collaborative structures should have access to professional development

centered on team-building activities, including the development of expectations, norms, roles, goals, strategies, and standards for success.

- The group should hold itself accountable for its work. The identification of goals, expectations, and standards is a necessary but not sufficient condition for the team to hold itself accountable. The development of self-accountable and monitoring collaborative structures is akin to the development of student-centered classrooms. Administrators should convey to the group that they value its work by supporting it without much interference. They should encourage the group to generate its own accountability measures and negotiate them if these appear to be insufficient or peripheral to the work.

CURRICULUM AND ASSESSMENT DESIGN WORK

In Chapter 2, I described the purposes and value of standards-based and learner-centered curriculum and assessment work. This work can be the focus of individual and/or collaborative work. Ideally, it should be grounded in a thorough analysis of curriculum and assessment gaps as well as in an exploration of areas of student learning that could be strengthened. The summer months offer an excellent opportunity for the initial drafting of units and assessments, given that much of this work requires 3 to 10 days of design time. Engaging in this work during the year is often compromised because of the fragmentation of the school calendar and the difficulties of securing large blocks of time.

In addition to providing teachers with initial design time, it is important for administrators and staff developers to identify the quality control and feedback procedures that teachers can use to analyze, revise, and expand upon their work. In-house staff developers, administrators, or teachers who are interested in curriculum review can play the role of reviewers and responders to teachers' work. Time for these procedures to be implemented and for the revision process should be secured during the year.

Finally, internally developed standards-based work should be discussed, shared, adapted, and revised by teachers who did not develop the work but can use it. Administrators could also use the work designed as a vehicle for establishing future curriculum design priorities or textbook review processes.

INQUIRY AND ANALYSIS WORK

Schools can benefit greatly from the collaborative use of data on teaching and learning. One of the ways in which administrators can develop learning communities and collegial structures is by involving teachers as true participants in the exploration of ways in which the school can be improved. The strategic and systematic use of data is essential in this endeavor. In Chapter 3, I have described three different approaches to using data, namely individual, collaborative, and school based. Each of these approaches has its own merit.

Following are some initial steps in engaging teachers in inquiry and data analysis:

1. Use surveys, interviews, and faculty, departmental, grade-level, or other meetings to identify and prioritize key teaching and student needs.

2. Share findings from shared decision-making teams or other school structures that underscore a major issue or problem in need of attention.

3. Offer teachers the opportunity to explore an issue or problem in depth individually or collaboratively (as an alternative to standard evaluation procedure, for credit, or as a release from other responsibilities).

4. Provide needed resources in the form of data, data analysis, professional development, books, or technical support to teachers who are willing and committed to inquiry.

5. Create one or more forums for the discussion, analysis, review, and use of findings obtained by the individual teachers or groups engaged in inquiry.

PROFESSIONAL PORTFOLIO WORK

There are many reasons to encourage teaching and administrative staff to develop and use professional portfolios. Among these are (a) the increased depth and validity of the evidence that can be obtained from beginning teachers who ultimately will go through a tenure review; (b) the value of professional portfolios as reflective tools that can assist teachers and administrators to slow down the pace of their work and study the impact of their decisions, their goals, and the merits and shortcomings of their work; and (c) the importance of documenting the expertise in the school, especially given periods in which there is a high incidence of retirements and influx of new staff.

As has been discussed in Chapter 4, portfolios can help document the history of expertise within the school and do much to document and consolidate best practices and the culture of the school.

To begin this process, administrative staff may select among the many purposes and audiences for portfolios and encourage a specific group of teachers or administrators to experiment with them. What is most important in the initial efforts is to provide time and to create a safe environment where teachers and administrators are free to share, analyze, and discuss possible entries.

Administrators may also consider encouraging individual or small groups of teachers to pursue National Certification or other formal leadership development activities, such as the ones provided by CSETL. The portfolios developed by these teachers can be shared and discussed among staff to identify sections in the portfolio requirements that can serve the needs of other subsets of teachers.

Developing the internal capacity of a school to become a learning community and to harness and use its own expertise is a long-term process requiring a sustained commitment on the part of many. This process can be greatly enhanced by the enacted beliefs and practices of administrative staff, such as (a) a belief that teachers are professionals and have all the rights and responsibilities that professionals have; (b) a belief that the school is a culture and that this culture is shaped by norms, expectations, values, myths, and a commitment to creating a shared culture that values leadership, reflection, inquiry, and shared decision making; and (c) a commitment to nurturing, developing, using, and sharing teachers' expertise.

The operationalization of these beliefs and practices may well take the form of standards-based and learner-centered design, professional portfolios, and/or systematic inquiry. Schools may end up relying on one of these methods, or they may use them all.

Appendix A: Description of CSETL and Its Mission

CSETL (pronounced "settle") is the acronym for the Center for the Study of Expertise in Teaching and Learning. Since its inception in 1995, CSETL has offered selected teachers, administrators, and staff developers an intellectually rigorous professional forum for collaborative research, the articulation of best practices, and the publication of exemplary instructional materials. CSETL fosters educational leadership among school practitioners and empowers educators to respond to the complex dynamics of educational reform. Other than the National Board for Teacher Certification, CSETL is the only existing nonprofit organization in the United States dedicated to the identification, articulation, and dissemination of teaching expertise.

CSETL HISTORY

CSETL is a nonprofit research and development center founded in 1995 by Dr. Giselle Martin-Kniep as a result of 12 years as a school reform researcher and consultant, working closely with school practitioners in the areas of organizational change, standards-based curriculum and assessment, and teacher-directed research.

Originally a vision shared by a handful of committed consultants, scholars, and practitioners, CSETL has now become a sought-after consortium for school reform deeply engrained in the culture of 16 New York school districts. What began as a primarily suburban initiative is currently also an integral component of the life of four inner-city school districts (Community School District 10 in New York City, Manhattan High Schools, Mt. Vernon City Schools in New York, and Buffalo City Schools). Originally a forum for elementary and secondary classroom teachers, CSETL now embraces school administrators, staff developers, special education, and English as a Second Language (ESL) coordinators.

CSETL has dramatically diversified the educator and student populations it serves. Its impact is also felt beyond the immediate community of its own fellows. Since its founding in 1995, CSETL has

1. Mentored 50 CSETL fellows in several suburban, rural, and urban school districts

2. Designed, field-tested, and published 18 exemplary standards-based curriculum and assessment units used by more than 10,000 educators across the United States and in selected international schools

3. Crafted and implemented over 30 professional development programs

4. Designed and carried out a variety of action research studies

5. Sponsored six annual conferences in which CSETL fellows showcase their expertise; the last two conferences were held in New York City and were cosponsored by the City University of New York Graduate Center

CSETL MISSION STATEMENT

The expertise of teachers has been minimally documented and therefore is not accessible to those who need it the most, their fellow teachers. Unlike other professionals, such as those in medicine and law, teachers do not currently assume a role in the preparation and certification of people who share their profession. In fact, there is a great distance between theory and practice regarding teaching and learning. Those who teach teachers may or may not have taught previously in elementary or secondary schools. Furthermore, teachers generally work in isolation and do not have sufficient opportunities to share what they know with each other. CSETL's intent is to provide teachers with a professional forum for collaborative research, development, and reflection.

Having a cadre of experienced teachers with a demonstrable record of success and leadership will allow the educational research and policy-making communities to explore previously untapped sources for maximizing teacher effectiveness, expertise, and resources. The guiding vision of CSETL is that it will provide schools with solid instructional leaders and exemplary instructional materials that can, in turn, help *improve schools from within.*

In summary, CSETL's focus is to improve teaching and learning in schools by addressing vital and currently unmet needs:

1. To identify, articulate, and record the collective "best practice" knowledge and insights that experienced teachers, students, researchers, and school administrators have about successful teaching and learning

2. To consolidate and widely disseminate the "best practices" used by expert educational practitioners

3. To help schools and districts identify, foster, and ultimately use their own teachers' expertise to produce schoolwide improvements in teaching and learning

Appendix B:
Unit Design Template

Center for the Study of
Expertise in Teaching and Learning

Standards-Based Design

Indicators

- What does each outcome/ standard look like?
- What does each mean in my classroom/subject/grade?
- What will students produce if they are working to attain the outcomes/ standards?

Outcomes/Standards

- What do I want students to know and be able to do?

Assessment

- What do I need to collect or administer to prove that students have grown toward and/or achieved desired outcomes/standards?

Essential Questions

- What compelling questions could I pose to students to focus my teaching and drive their inquiry and learning?

Performance Criteria/Rubrics

- How will I communicate what mastery or accomplishment means?
- What does quality mean for me and my students?
- How good is good enough?

Learning Opportunities

- What do I need to teach or have students experience so that they will attain the learning outcomes/ standards?
- What concepts/skills/ processes are needed?

Checklist of Unit Components

Organizing Center
Preliminary Description of Unit
Professional Context Statement
Unit Context
Overview
Rationale
Outcomes/Standards
Essential Questions
Guiding Questions
Reflective Questions
Culminating Authentic Assessment
Diagnostic Assessment
Learning Opportunities/Unit Sketch
Formative Assessment
Performance Criteria
Resources
Supplementary Resources
Reflective Statement

Selected Organizing Center for the Unit

Can be a concept, issue, problem, or essential question

Preliminary Description of Unit

This section allows the author to brainstorm ideas that may later fit into the rationale, context, or introduction of the unit. The section will not be part of the published unit but should be kept until the unit is finished, since sometimes the author may want to revisit initial thoughts.

Professional Context Statement

This section addresses the following questions to the author: What do you do professionally? Where? With whom? When are you doing the work you are planning to do for your unit? With whom? For how long?

Unit Context

The unit context provides information on a) the target audience for the unit; b) its fit into the curriculum for a grade or subject, and c) prerequisite content and skills.

Overview

The unit overview or introduction provides a synopsis of the unit and addresses questions such as:

What is the scope of the unit? What knowledge, skills, or dispositions (values) does the unit target? What major standards does it address? How is the unit structured? What questions does it address? What are its major components? How long does it take?

Rationale

The unit rationale justifies the unit's existence and value by addressing the following questions: Why is this unit important? How will students benefit or become better people? What will they learn?

Outcomes/Standards

Outcomes are statements that describe what the teacher wants students to know, be able to do, or value as a result of engaging with the unit. Standards are similar statements but are generated by groups of people at the district, state, or national levels. Because standards may not include all kinds of outcomes statements, it is important for teachers to be able to generate their own list.

In this template, teachers articulate their outcomes as well as desired state and national standards in the section below. These outcomes and standards are subdivided into those that will be taught but not formally assessed (because they have already been or will be formally assessed in other units) and those that will be taught and formally assessed.

As a result of this unit, students will:

Know/Understand	*Do*	*Value*
Applicable state and national standards that will be **taught**	Applicable state and national standards that will be **taught**	Applicable state and national standards that will be **taught**
Applicable state and national standards that will be **assessed**	Applicable state and national standards that will be **assessed**	Applicable state and national standards that will be **assessed**

Essential Questions

Essential questions are used to hook the students into the unit, to stimulate inquiry, and to maintain students' interest throughout it. In this section, the author identifies a compelling question that will be used as the organizing center for the unit.

Guiding Questions

Guiding questions support the unit structure (prior knowledge, knowledge acquisition, synthesis, transfer) and allow the author to connect lessons and to make the unit or learning event as cohesive as possible.

Reflective Questions

Reflective questions support students' metacognitive processes and allow them to reflect on different aspects related to learning. These include the processes they used to learn (e.g., "How did you solve that problem?"), the merits and shortcomings of their products and performance (e.g., "What is the best part of your essay?"), their feelings and thoughts as learners (e.g., "What aspects of this work are you finding most challenging?"), and their learning as a whole (e.g., "What is the most important thing you learned this week?"). These questions support the transfer component of the unit structure.

Culminating Authentic Assessment

The culminating authentic assessment serves as a summative evaluation of the unit. It enables students to synthesize what they have learned by engaging in a real-world performance or developing a product for an audience that can benefit from the work. This assessment corresponds to the synthesis component of the unit structure.

Diagnostic Assessment

Diagnostic assessments are measures, tasks, or problems given to students at the beginning of the unit to ascertain their prior knowledge, skills, or attitudes. These address the initial component of the unit structure.

Learning Opportunities/Unit Sketch

Learning opportunities include lessons or activities that the teacher will use to engage students in learning. These need to consider a number of criteria, including (a) sensitivity to multiple learning styles and intelligences in terms of students' both accessing material and demonstrating what they know; (b) rich use of literature; (c) inquiry questions and experiences throughout the unit; (d) flexibility and choice in terms of specific activities or experiences within a lesson or assessment; (e) academic rigor; and (f) incorporation of basic and higher-order thinking skills.

The unit sketch enables authors to list their learning experiences and other unit components.

Unit Sketch: Map of Learning Opportunities/Lessons/Activities

Learning opportunities should:

- Address multiple intelligences and learning styles
- Be literature rich
- Be inquiry based
- Offer flexibility/choice
- Be rigorous
- Incorporate both basic and higher-level thinking skills

Assessments can be:

Recall-based
Performance-based
Product-based
Process-based (reflections)

	Monday	Tuesday	Wednesday	Thursday	Friday
Guiding questions					
Learning opportunities include reflective prompts					
Formal assessments Specify: • Diagnostic • Formative • Summative Specify: • Individual • Group					
Standards and Indicators					

Formative Assessment

Formative assessments are checks for understanding or skill attainment that teachers use between lessons or at different points within the unit to determine where students are as learners.

Performance Criteria

Explicit performance criteria should support all summative assessments and some, if not all, diagnostic assessments. These criteria stem directly from the standards and performance indicators that drive the unit.

Students should know and understand teacher expectations via checklists, rubrics, or other scales. The teacher should also consider developing or identifying exemplars (samples of exemplary performances or products) and anchors (samples of contrasting work) to support their checklists and rubrics.

A chart for rubrics is included below.

SCORING RUBRIC

Resources					
Print		Video/Media		Audio	
Teacher	Student Handouts Literature	Teacher	Student	Teacher	Student
Supplementary Resources and Bibliographies					

Reflective Statement

In writing the unit, authors should consider questions such as the following: How did you go about writing this? What stages did you experience? How difficult was to for you to complete this? What did you learn about yourself in writing this? What did you struggle with? What would you do differently if you could?

Appendix C: Application to Become a CSETL Fellow

CSETL fellows engage in a number of activities that enable them to understand, document, and validate their educational expertise. Over the course of their fellowship, they document their growth and achievement related to four different outcomes:

- Understanding and use of learner-centered curriculum and assessment
- Ability to present oneself as a professional
- Use of reflection to improve upon practice
- Commitment and willingness to share expertise

The documentation of these outcomes begins with the application process, which initially assumes the form of a baseline portfolio and evolves into a certification portfolio.

APPLICATION PROCESS

1. In general, it is recommended that applicants have a minimum of 3 years of school/classroom experience.

2. Applications are reviewed throughout the year and need to be submitted before the first CSETL session in the fall.

3. Prior to submitting their application, applicants will have the opportunity to engage in a conversation with a CSETL staff member and fellow. This conversation will allow the applicant to ask questions about CSETL and explore what the fellowship is about.

4. Accepted applicants will also attend a formal orientation session prior to the fall program, at which time they will be welcomed as probationary fellows.

5. Probationary fellows will work with an assigned mentor to complete a baseline portfolio that will move them from probationary status to fellowship status. The mentor will help them determine their interests, needs, strengths, learning style, etc.

6. The baseline portfolio should be submitted to CSETL at 20 Elm Place, Sea Cliff, NY 11579 before the January session of the probationary fellow's first year.

APPLICATION

The application to CSETL consists of a "dear reader" letter that includes

- A description of who the applicant is and what he or she does (context)
- A statement of what the applicant values as an educator in the form of a statement of a philosophy of learning or teaching or a vision for schools
- An analysis of professional strengths and weaknesses
- Goals for professional work
- An explanation of the applicant's motivation for becoming a CSETL fellow and his or her expectations of the fellowship experience
- A **Baseline Portfolio** that includes the following entries:
  a. Two letters of recommendation, one of which is written by a supervisor. The other letter may be replaced by an observation that documents the applicant's strengths or talents.
  b. An annotated learning experience/lesson sample of best practice that shows the applicant's achievements as an educator with an accompanying reflection. The learning experience and its reflective annotation can be on text, video, or other media. The reflection should reveal the applicant's ability to reflect on his or her professional practice.
  c. A résumé that includes evidence of participation in and/or facilitation of professional development activities.

Appendix D: Professional Portfolio Rubric

Dimension	Resident Fellowship Candidate	Meets Certification Requirements	Developed but Needs Revision	Emerging
Understands and can use learner-centered curriculum and assessment	Portfolio includes varied and impressive samples of student-centered curriculum that – Are inquiry based, rigorous, standards based, meaningful, and integrated in more than one way – Demand critical thinking through use of essential and guiding questions and inductive and deductive reasoning about real problems – Embed diversified diagnostic, formative, and summative assessments and authentic products and performances that measure application and knowledge throughout the learning process	Portfolio includes varied samples of student-centered curriculum that – Are standards based, meaningful, and interdisciplinary – Demand higher-order thinking through the use of application and/or open-ended questions – Include varied diagnostic and summative assessments, products, and performances as well as recall-based tests – Use standards-based criteria in teacher-developed checklists and rubrics – Provide students with the opportunity to reflect and	Portfolio includes samples of curriculum that – Are standards based and focus on a single discipline or on parallel disciplines – Require recall, comprehension, and factual knowledge acquisition through the use of open- and close-ended questions – Include limited summative products and performances as well as recall-based tests – Use explicit criteria in checklists and rubrics	Portfolio includes samples of curriculum that – Are not directly connected to standards or focus primarily on skills within a single discipline – Focus on recall of isolated knowledge, skills, and/or facts through the use of close-ended questions – Rely on traditional, recall-based tests as primary means of assessment – Lack explicit performance criteria – Preclude student reflection and self-assessment.

(Continued)

Dimension	Resident Fellowship Candidate	Meets Certification Requirements	Developed but Needs Revision	Emerging
	– Involve students in the development and use of standards-based criteria in checklists and rubrics – Provide ongoing and varied opportunities for student reflection, self-assessment, and revision	self-assess at the beginning and end of the learning process	– Provide students with the opportunity to self- or peer- assess at some point in the learning process	
Demonstrates the ability to present oneself as a professional	Candidate creates a unique, focused, and clear portfolio that showcases expertise and provides a rich, multifaceted portrayal of the professional Portfolio has a unifying theme, metaphor, or question that ties all the pieces together Candidate skillfully incorporates technology, media, or art into the portfolio presentation	Candidate creates a focused and clear portfolio that shows several professional sides or angles Portfolio is organized logically, making it clear and easy to read Candidate effectively includes aspects of technology, media, or art to enhance the portfolio presentation	Candidate creates a focused portfolio that shows a single professional side Placement and order of entries cause questions for the reader related to the nature or meaning of the work and require further explanation to be clear Candidate effectively uses a single medium of communication	Candidate creates an unfocused collection of work The order and content of the collection is confusing/illogical and creates questions for the reader about the work and its author Candidate relies on a single medium of communication that may be inappropriate or used ineffectively
Uses reflection to improve upon practice	Portfolio includes varied, insightful, and reflective documents/artifacts that reveal – Thorough and systematic analysis of process and meaning of own work – Accurate use of data to draw conclusions, make decisions, set goals, and generate questions for study – Identification of specific strengths and areas for	Portfolio includes reflective documents/ artifacts that reveal – Systematic analysis of value and process of own work – Accurate use of data to draw conclusions and make decisions related to own work – Identification of strengths and areas for	Portfolio includes reflective documents/ artifacts that reveal – General analysis of meaning or quality of own work – A collection of data with no analysis or purposeful connection to own work – Identification of general	Portfolio includes descriptive documents/artifacts that reveal – The kind of work done – Missing data or inclusion of data that are misrepresented or irrelevant to work – Description of process and struggles related to work without supporting documents

(Continued)

Dimension	Resident Fellowship Candidate	Meets Certification Requirements	Developed but Needs Revision	Emerging
	improvement, supported with perceptive references to own work – Descriptions of specific strategies for improving areas in need – Setting and monitoring of both short- and long-term goals in ways that are likely to measure changes in attainment or expertise	improvement, supported with specific references to own work – Explanation of possible strategies for improving areas in need – Setting and monitoring of realistic short-term goals or of a long-term goal with accompanying supporting benchmarks	strengths and areas for improvement without tangible supporting documentation – Outline of general plan for improving areas in need – Setting of realistic short-term goals that may not be directly related to or supported by work	– Plan for improvements sketchy or missing – General, vague statements of future goals
Demonstrates a commitment and willingness to share expertise	Portfolio includes documents/ artifacts that – Demonstrate a clear commitment to develop CSETL as an organization – Describe, analyze, and evaluate various efforts to share expertise in different contexts and with different audiences – Illustrate the process and results of shared expertise by showcasing samples of own work, as well as other teachers' work – Analyze specific strengths and areas for improvement supported by references to work – Identify future goals and strategies for improving this work and for further sharing expertise	Portfolio includes documents/ artifacts that – Demonstrate a willingness to enhance the work of CSETL – Describe various efforts to share expertise in a single context – Show the process of sharing expertise by showcasing samples of own work – Identify specific strengths and areas for improvement in work – Identify future goals for sharing expertise	Portfolio includes documents/ artifacts that – Show learning and work produced in CSETL – List various efforts to share expertise informally – Show that expertise was shared by including descriptions of work – Identify general strengths and/or weaknesses in work – List potential methods of sharing expertise without specific goals or plans for implementing them	Portfolio includes documents/ artifacts that – Appear to be unfinished or works in progress or show work unrelated to participation in CSETL – Reveal a lack of interest in sharing expertise or an inability to share it – List work accomplished – Present own work without reference to the strengths or weaknesses revealed by the work – Make no reference to plans for sharing expertise

References

Allen, D. (Ed.). (1998). *Assessing student learning: From grading to understanding.* New York: Teachers College Press.

Argyris, C., & Schon, D. (1978). *Organizational learning: A theory of action perspective.* San Francisco: Jossey-Bass.

Bain, H. P., & Jacobs, R. (1990, September). The case for smaller classes and better teachers. *Streamlined Seminar: National Association of Elementary School Principals, 9*(1).

Bernhardt, V. (1998). *Data analysis for comprehensive schoolwide improvement.* Larchmont, NY: Eye on Education.

Blythe, T., Allen, D., & Powell, B. S. (1999). *Looking together at student work: A companion guide to "Assessing student learning."* New York: Teachers College Press.

Boud, D., Keogh, R., & Walker, D. (Eds.). (1985). *Reflection: Turning experience into learning.* London: Kogan Page.

Boud, D., & Walker, D. (1998). Promoting reflection in professional courses: The challenge of context. *Studies in Higher Education, 23*(2), 191–206.

Brophy, J., & Good, T. L. (1986). Teacher behavior and student achievement. In M. C. Wittrock (Ed.), *Handbook of research on teaching* (3rd ed., pp. 328–371). New York: Macmillan.

Carini, P. (2001). *Starting strong: A different look at children, schools, and standards.* New York: Teachers College Press.

Collinson, V., Killeavy, M., & Stephenson, H. J. (1999). Exemplary teachers: Practicing an ethic of care in England, Ireland, and the United States. *Journal for a Just and Caring Education, 5*(4), 349–366.

Combs, A. W., Miser, A. B., & Whitaker, K. S. (1999). *On becoming a school leader: A person-centered challenge.* Alexandria, VA: Association for Supervision and Curriculum Development.

Covino, E. A., & Iwanicki, E. (1996). Experienced teachers: Their constructs on effective teaching. *Journal of Personnel Evaluation in Education, 11,* 325–363.

Cruickshank, D. R., & Haefele, D. (2001). Good teachers, plural. *Educational Leadership, 58*(5), 26–30.

Danielson, C., & McGreal, T. (2000). *Teacher evaluation: To enhance professional practice.* Alexandria, VA: Association for Supervision and Curriculum Development.

Demmon-Berger, D. (1986). *Effective teaching: Observations from research.* Arlington, VA: American Association of School Administrators.

Doyle, W., & Ponder, G. (1977). The practical ethic and teacher decision-making. *Interchange, 8*(3), 1–12.

DuFour, R., & Eaker, R. (1998). *Professional learning communities at work: Best practices for enhancing student achievement.* Alexandria, VA: Association for Supervision and Curriculum Development.

Eastwood, K., & Lewis, K. (1992). Restructuring that lasts: Managing the performance dip. *Journal of School Leadership, 2*(2), 213–214.

Fullan, M. (1994). Teacher leadership: A failure to conceptualize. In D. Walling (Ed.), *Teachers as leaders: Perspectives on the professional development of teachers* (pp. 241–253). Bloomington, IN: Phi Delta Kappa Educational Foundation.

Glickman, S. (2002). *How does classroom assessment practice affect student writing?* Unpublished manuscript.

Guskey, T. (1986). Staff development and the process of teacher change. *Educational Researcher, 15*(5), 5–12.

Guskey, T., & Sparks, D. (1996, Fall). Exploring the relationship between staff development and improvements in student learning. *Journal of Staff Development, 17*(4), 4–37.

Jacobs, H. H. (1997). *Mapping the big picture: Integrating curriculum and assessment K–12.* Alexandria, VA: Association for Supervision and Curriculum Development.

Kouzes, J. M., & Posner, B. Z. (1999). *Encouraging the heart: A leader's guide to rewarding and recognizing others.* San Francisco: Jossey-Bass

Little, J. W. (1981). *School success and staff development: The role of staff development in urban desegregated schools. Executive summary.* Washington, DC: National Institute of Education.

Louis, K. S., Kruse, S., & Marks, H. (1996). Schoolwide professional community. In Fred Newmann & Associates (Eds.), *Authentic achievement: Restructuring schools for intellectual quality* (pp. 179–203). San Francisco: Jossey-Bass.

Marantz Cohen, R. (2002, March). Schools our teachers deserve: A proposal for teacher-centered reform. *Phi Delta Kappan,* 532–37.

Martin-Kniep, G. (1999). *Capturing the wisdom of practice: Professional portfolios for educators.* Alexandria, VA: Association for Supervision and Curriculum Development.

Martin-Kniep, G. (2000). *Becoming a better teacher: Eight innovations that work.* Alexandria, VA: Association for Supervision and Curriculum Development.

Marzano, R., Pickering, D., & McTighe, J. (1993). *Assessing student outcomes.* Alexandria, VA: Association for Supervision and Curriculum Development.

Mitchell, R. D. (1998). World class teachers: When top teachers earn National Board Certification, schools—and students— reap the benefits. *American School Board Journal, 185*(9), 27–29.

Newmann, F., & Associates (1996). *Authentic achievement: Restructuring schools for intellectual quality.* San Francisco: Jossey-Bass.

Newmann, F. W., Secada, W. G., & Wehlage, G. G. (1995). *A guide to authentic instruction and assessment: Vision, standards and scoring.* Madison: Wisconsin Center for Education Research.

Noffke, S. E., & Stevenson, R. B. (1995). *Educational action research: Becoming practically critical.* New York: Teachers College Press.

Rowan, B., Chiang, F. S., & Miller, R. (1997). Using research on employees' performance to study the effects of teachers on student achievement. *Sociology of Education, 70,* 256–284.

Seidel, S. (1998). Wondering to be done: The Collaborative Assessment Conference. In D. Allen (Ed.), *Assessing student learning: From grading to understanding.* New York: Teachers College Press.

Sergiovanni, T., & Starratt, R. (1979). *Supervision: Human perspectives.* New York: McGraw-Hill.

Snell, J., & Swanson, J. (2000, April). *The essential knowledge and skills of teacher leaders: A search for a conceptual framework.* Paper presented at the annual meeting of the American Educational Research Association, New Orleans.

Stiegler, J. W., & Herbert, J. (1999). *The teaching gap: Best ideas for the world's teachers for improving education in the classroom.* New York: Free Press.

Stiggins, R. J. (1994). *Student-centered classroom assessment.* New York: Merrill.

Stronge, J. H. (2002). *Qualities of effective teachers.* Alexandria, VA: Association for Supervision and Curriculum Development.

Swanson, J. (2000, April). *What differentiates an excellent teacher from a teacher leader?* Paper presented at the annual meeting of the American Educational Research Association, New Orleans.

Thomas, J. A., & Montgomery, P. (1998). On becoming a good teacher: Reflective practice with regard to children's voices. *Journal of Teacher Education, 49,* 372–380.

Thorpe, M. (2000). Encouraging students to reflect as part of the assignment process. *Active Learning in Higher Education, 1*(1), 79–92.

Wiggins, G. (1998). *Educative assessment: Designing assessments to inform and improve student performance.* San Francisco: Jossey-Bass.

Wiggins, G., & McTighe, J. (1998). *Understanding by design.* Alexandria, VA: Association for Supervision and Curriculum Dvelopment.

Wright, S. P., Horn, S. P., & Sanders, W. (1997). Teacher and classroom context effects on student achievement: Implications for teacher evaluation. *Journal of Personnel Evaluation in Education, 11,* 57–67.

Index

Page references followed by *t* indicate a table;
followed by *b* indicate a boxed figure;
followed by *fig* indicate an illustrated figure.

Action plan
    assessment of needs, 79-80
    brokering of relationships among teachers, 80-81
    curriculum/assessment design work, 81
    identifying internal expertise, 79
    inquiry and analysis work, 81-82
    professional portfolio work, 82
Action research: An educational leader's guide to
        school improvement (Glanz), 57
Action research
    on collaborative inquiry in ELA, 44-47*t*, 48-50*t*, 51
    on individual inquiry in ELA, 39-40*t*, 41-44*t*
    learning community development using, 81-82
    recommended books on, 57-58
    role in professional identity development of
        teachers, 37
    on school-based inquiry in ELA, 51-55, 52*t*
Administrators
    encouraging teachers to pursue development
        activities, 82
    learning community support by, 11-13
    See also Schools; Teachers
Allen, D., 5, 13, 57
American Museum of Natural History (New York),
        17, 18
Atkinson, J., 51
Authentic assessment: A collection (Burke), 32
Authentic assessment: A handbook for educators
        (Hart), 33

Bedell, E., 17, 23
Belanoff, P., 76
Bernhardt, V., 37, 57
Black, L., 76
Blythe, T., 5, 13, 57
Boerum, L. J., 17
Burke, K., 32, 76
Burnaford, G., 57

Capturing the wisdom of practice: Professional
        portfolios for educators (Martin-Kniep), 77

Carini, P., 5
Classroom based assessment (Hill & Norwick), 33
Coalition of Essential Schools, 16
Collaborative environment, as school improvement
        factor, 1
Collaborative inquiry
    assessment of student responses in
        pretests/posttests, 50*t*
    examples of student posttest, 48-49
    examples of student pretest, 46, 48, 49
    findings on student writing using, 49, 51
    number of words generated in pretests/
        posttests, 47*t*
    overview of, 44-46
Combs, A. W., 1, 13, 67
Community School District 10 (Bronx), 39
Creating integrated curriculum (Drake), 32
"Critical friends" peer review, 12*t*
CSETL (Center for the Study of Expertise in Teaching
        and Learning)
    application to become CSETL fellow, 95-96
    group formation component of, 4
    history of, 83-84
    mentoring process used in, 4-5
    mission statement of, 84
    origins of, 1-2
    outcomes-based rubric for certification portfolio,
        61*t*-62*t*
    professional development programs offered
        through, 6*t*-11*t*, 12*t*
    standards-based curriculum/assessment
        prototypes facilitated by, 3
    teacher research activities encouraged by, 5
CSETL fellow application, 97-98
Curriculum. *See* Standards-based curriculum
Cutchogue East Elementary School (Long Island), 2

Dailker, D., 76
*Data analysis for comprehensive schoolwide
        improvement* (Bernhardt), 57
Data-driven inquiry
    categories of, 37-38
    example of collaborative, 44-47*t*, 48-50*t*, 51
    example of individual, 39-40*t*, 41-44*t*
    example of school-based, 51-55, 52*t*

learning community development using, 81-82
questions for reader on, 56
recommended books on, 57-58
role in professional identity development of
teachers, 37
school support of each type of, 56
"Dear reader" letters (excerpts), 67t, 72t
Designing professional portfolios for change (Burke), 76
Dickson, M., 76
Doyle, W., 2
Drake, S., 32
DuFour, R., 13, 15, 80

Eaker, R., 13, 15, 80
Eastwood, K., 1
Educational action research: Becoming practically critical
(Noffke & Stevenson), 57
*Educative assessment: Designing assessments to inform
and improve student performance* (Wiggins), 34
ELA (English language arts)
collaborative inquiry used in, 44-47t, 48-50t, 51
individual inquiry used in, 39-40t, 41-44t
rubric for writing response for, 40t
school-based inquiry used in, 51-55, 52t
student preparation for testing of, 39
Ellis, A. K., 32
"Expertise" (16-week second-grad unit)
overview of, 16-19
partial rubric from, 27t
partial sketch of, 21t
similarities with other units, 20, 22-24, 26
student journals kept in, 24-26b

Fischer, J., 57

GEMS (Gateway to Educational Material Science), 19
Genesee Valley Board of Cooperative Educational
Services (New York), 51
Glanz, J., 57
Glickman, S., 39, 41, 55
Gordon, P., 13
Graves, D. H., 76
Green, J. E., 76
Growth artifacts, 60, 62, 65
*A guide to authentic instruction and assessment: Vision,
standards and scoring* (Newmann, Secada, &
Wehlage), 34
Guskey, T., 2

Hart, D., 33
Herbert, J., 1
Hill, C., 33
Hirsh, S., 14
Hobsen, D., 57
Home page of Web-based portfolio, 73*fig*
How to help beginning teachers succeed (Gordon &
Maxey), 13

Individual inquiry
David's reflections predicting test scores, 44

David's revised writing sample of, 43-44
overview of, 39-44
rubric for writing response for English Language
Arts, 40t
students' self-self-evaluation sheet for writing
sample, 44t
The interdisciplinary curriculum (Ellis & Stuen), 32

Jacobs, H. H., 16, 33

Kouzes, J. M., 1, 37, 56
Kuhn, T., 33

"Laws of Science" (7-week sixth-grade unit)
hypotheses formed by students during, 24-26
overview of, 17, 19-20
partial rubric from, 28t
partial sketch of, 22t
similarities with other units, 20, 22-24, 26
student events journal, 23-25b
Learning communities
action plan for developing, 79-82
activities of, 3
barriers to development of, 7, 11
describing/defining, 1-2
importance of, 2
range of activities/requirements for engaging, 2-7
recommended books on, 13-14
supporting, 11-13
Lewis, K., 1
*Looking together at student work: A companion guide to
"Assessing student learning"* (Blythe, Allen, &
Powell), 13, 57
Lynch, P., 16

McTighe, J., 16, 30, 34
Manhasset Public Schools (Long Island), 16
*Mapping the big picture: Integrating curriculum and
assessment K-12* (Jacobs), 33
Martin-Kniep, G., 16, 72, 77
Marzano, R., 16, 30
Mathematics assessment: Alternative approaches
(Kuhn), 33
Maxey, S., 13
Mentees, 4
Mentoring process
CSETL use of, 4
establishing between new/veteran teachers, 5
Mentors, 4
Miller, B., 33
Miser, A. B., 1, 13

Needs assessment, 79-80
New directions in portfolio assessment (Black, Daiker,
Summers, & Stygall), 76
A new vision for staff development (Hirsh & Sparks), 14
New York State Informational Systems Standard, 18
New York State Language Arts Standards, 18, 20
New York State Mathematics, Science and
Technology Standards, 18, 20

New York State Science Standards, 18
Newmann, F. W., 16, 34
Noffke, S. E., 37, 57
Norwick, L., 33

On becoming a school leader: A person-centered
    challenge (Combs, Miser, & Whitaker), 13

Peer review protocol, 12t
Performance assessment in the social studies classroom:
    A how-to book for teachers (McCollum), 33
Pickering, D., 16
Ponder, G., 2
Portfolio portraits (Graves & Sunstein), 76
Portfolios: Process and product (Belanoff &
    Dickson), 76
Posner, B. Z., 1, 37, 56
Powell, B. S., 5, 13, 57
Preparing citizens: Linking authentic assessment and
    instruction in civic/law-related education (Miller &
    Singleton), 33
Professional development presentations
    examples of CSETL teacher workshops, 6t-7
    protocol for peer review of, 12t
    rubric for programs and, 8t-11t
    self-assessment rubric for program
        participants, 11t
Professional learning communities at work: Best
    practices for enhancing student achievement
    (DuFour & Eaker), 13
Professional portfolios
    components of, 60
    described, 59
    different images/frameworks of, 70fig, 71fig,
        72fig, 73fig
    as frameworks documenting professional
        expertise, 59-60
    home page for a Web-based, 73fig
    learning community development using, 82
    ongoing reflective process used in, 66-68, 69t
    organization of, 69-73, 75
    outcomes and artifacts strategies used in, 74t
    outcomes-based rubric for CSETL certification,
        61t-62t
    possible questions for reader on, 76
    recommended books on, 76-77
    rubric for, 97-99
    school support of development/use of, 75
    showcase and growth artifacts appropriate for,
        60, 62, 65
Professional portfolios entries
    analysis of laboratory experiment, 68t
    depiction of two tasks/analysis, 65t
    description/analysis of curriculum, 63t
    designing learning opportunities, 64t
    excerpts from "Dear Reader" letters, 67t, 72t
    on portfolios and understanding, 74t
    reflection on continuing on path toward well-
        developed, 66
    on the struggle of portfolio work, 74t

three needs and goals statements, 69t
two educational platforms, 68t
two examples of use of reflection to improve one's
    teaching, 69t

"A Quiet Garden" (4-week ninth-grade earth
    science unit)
    overview of, 17, 20
    partial rubric from, 29t
    partial sketch of, 23t
    similarities with other units, 20, 22-24, 26
    students responses to reflective questions
        during, 26

Reflection
    continuing on the path toward well-developed
        unit, 66t
    to improve one's practice, 66-68
    two examples for improving one's teaching, 69t

Sag Harbor Public Schools (Long Island), 17
School-based inquiry
    overview of, 51-55
    school support of, 56
    summary of fourth-grade test demands, 52t
    teacher reflection on process of, 55
Schools
    collaborative environment and improvement
        initiatives of, 1
    identifying internal expertise within, 79
    professional portfolios development/use support
        by, 75
    support of data-driven inquiry/action
        research by, 56
    See also Administrators; Teachers
Secada, W. G., 34
Seidel, S., 5
Sergiovanni, T., 67
Showcase artifacts, 60
Singleton, L., 33
Smith, A., 2
Smyser, S. O., 76
Snell, J., 4
Sparks, D., 14
Standards-based curriculum
    common elements of, 20, 22-24, 26
    "Expertise," 16-19, 21t, 24, 26b, 27t
    helping teachers to develop high-quality, 30-32
    "Laws of Science," 17, 19-20, 22t, 23-25b, 28t
    "A Quiet Garden," 17, 20, 26, 29t
    showcase and growth artifacts showing use of,
        60, 62, 65
    what does it take to develop a, 29-30
Standards-based curriculum design
    components of, 16
    examining approach to, 15-16
    learning community development through, 81
    questions for the reader on, 32
    recommended books on, 32-34
    template for, 85-93

Starratt, R., 67
Stevenson, R. B., 37, 57
Stiegler, J. W., 1
Stiggins, R. J., 16, 34
Stronge, J. H., 2, 31, 66
Student-centered classroom assessment (Stiggins), 34
Stuen, C. J., 32
Stygall, G., 76
Summers, J., 76
Sunstein, B. S., 76
Swanson, J., 4

The teacher portfolio (Green & Smyser), 76
Teacher workshops (CSETL), 6t-7
Teachers
    brokering of relationships among, 80-81
    encouraged to pursue development activities, 82
    facilitating high-quality standards-based units by,
        30-32
    learning community support by, 11-13

ongoing reflective process used by, 66-68, 69t
    See also Administrators; Schools
Teachers doing research: Practical possibilities
    (Burnaford, Fischer, & Hobsen), 57
The Teaching Gap (Stiegler and Herbert), 1
Thorpe, M., 16

Understanding by design (Wiggins & McTighe), 34
Using data to improve student achievement
    (Wahlstrom), 58

Wahlstrom, D., 58
Web-based portfolio home page, 73*fig*
Wehlage, G. G., 34
Whitaker, K. S., 1, 13
Why am I doing this? (Martin-Kniep), 77
Wiggins, G., 16, 30, 34
William Floyd School District (Long Island), 17
Wright, S. P., 31

**CORWIN
PRESS**

The Corwin Press logo—a raven striding across an open book— represents the happy union of courage and learning. We are a professional-level publisher of books and journals for K-12 educators, and we are committed to creating and providing resources that embody these qualities. Corwin's motto is "Success for All Learners."